Having been Senior Partner and Head of Family Law Team at Pickerings (a Legal 500 practice) and having specialised in family law since the 1980s, Graham is now a consultant within the firm's Children Law team, representing children, parents, prospective parents and clinics in public and private law cases, with a special emphasis on care, adoption and surrogacy matters. He has presented training courses for solicitors, barristers and legal executives on a variety of children law subjects across the country for a number of training organisations since 1997.

A Practical Guide to Adoption for Family Lawyers

A Practical Guide to Adoption for Family Lawyers

Graham Pegg, LLB Hons, Solicitor

Law Brief Publishing

Published 2019 by Law Brief Publishing, an imprint of Law Brief Publishing Ltd
30 The Parks
Minehead
Somerset
TA24 8BT

www.lawbriefpublishing.com

Paperback: 978-1-912687-19-0

To Laura, Hayley and Steve, who have taught me what "family" actually means

PREFACE

There are very few court orders that actually change who a person is but an adoption order does just that. There can be no greater intrusion into Family Life by the State than for a court to make a placement order paving the way to the child ceasing to be a member of one family and, at a stroke, belonging to another. The pleasure of the adoption "celebration" – not so much a hearing more a photo opportunity – contrasts starkly with the agonising that precedes a parent deciding to "relinquish" a child for adoption, let alone with the devastation for the birth family of a court imposing that outcome after a bitterly contested hearing.

The 2002 Adoption and Children Act aimed to bring the law more into line with the, at the time, groundbreaking Children Act of 1989. Whether it really succeeded is a matter for debate – it certainly left one or two enigmas for the courts to resolve and by now most of them have been. But it brought into the legal lexicon some new concepts – placement for adoption, special guardianship and adoption by unmarried, possibly same-sex couples, to name but a few. Subsequent statutes and statutory instruments have carried out a bit of "fine tuning" and, of course, case law has developed apace.

This Practical Guide covers the range of processes in the Courts in England and Wales and in Local Authorities and other Adoption Agencies here that relate to the adoption of UK children, as at 31st October 2018. It includes how prospective adopters become approved, how a parent's wish for the child to be adopted is formalised, the placement for adoption route, the application to adopt and the effect of adoption orders. It also deals with the choice between adoption and special guardianship, applications to revoke placement orders or to join in and oppose adoption applications, step-parent adoption and the issue of contact after placement and adoption orders have been made.

Graham Pegg
December 2018

CONTENTS

Chapter One	Introduction – The Concept of Adoption	1
Chapter Two	The Adoption & Children Act 2002 Welfare Principle and Checklist	5
Chapter Three	The Adoption Application	13
	A. Who Can Apply to Adopt?	13
	B. Preliminaries to Adoption Applications	15
	C. Reports and Notices of Intention to Adopt	18
	D. The Application	21
Chapter Four	Approval of Applicants to Adopt	25
Chapter Five	Step-Parent, or Partner of Parent Adoption	29
Chapter Six	Illegality	33
Chapter Seven	Placement and Adoption with Parental Consent	37
	A. 6 Weeks After the Child's Birth	39
	B. Non-Disclosure by Mother of Identity of Father, etc	40
	C. Competence to Consent to Placement	44
	D. Parental Responsibility after Relinquishment	47
	E. Change of Mind by Parent or Agency	47
Chapter Eight	Placement Orders	51
	A. The Application	51
	B. The Effect of the Placement Order	55
	C. The Placement Order Itself	56
	D. Placement Timescales	58
Chapter Nine	Revocation of Placement Orders and Opposing Adoption	61
	A. Leave to Apply	61
	B. The Test of Change in Circumstances	64

Chapter Ten	The Adoption Order	75
Chapter Eleven	Adoption or Special Guardianship	79
Chapter Twelve	Adoption Support	87
Chapter Thirteen	Contact After Adoption or Placement Orders	95
	A. Contact During "Authority to Place"	95
	B. Post Adoption Contact	99

CHAPTER ONE
INTRODUCTION – THE CONCEPT OF ADOPTION

Perhaps we should not refer to those who are adopted as "adopted children", they are, in fact, adopted people. In ancient Rome, adults were often the subject of adoption, (the Emperor Augustus, adopted into the Caesar family at the age of 19, was probably the most famous example). In this country, once the adopted person has reached the age of 18, he or she cannot then be adopted again and so that is who this person is until death and, in fact, after death, for the purposes of inheritance and lineage.

So, it could be said, the adoption order is the longest lasting order a court can make in respect of a human being. It is, almost always, eternal.

Adoption is the recognition by a legal system of a piece of social rearrangement that verges on the fictional. The adopted person is treated as though born to the adopter(s) by the natural biological process. This degree of make believe is supposed to resolve some of the problems which surround the practice, common to many societies, human and animal, of rearing the offspring of another.

Adoption attempts to improve the cement between adopter and adoptee. The idea is that the adopted person views himself as an integral part of the adoptive family, feeling that this is his or her own family for life; providing a sense of "permanence" and belonging which is considered a fundamental building block for the development of a well-balanced personality. Adopters, in turn, are given, by the process, the feeling of certainty that no-one is going to turn up at their door, with or without the order of some court, and demand their child back.

But it is not a perfect fiction, nor is there any need for it to be fictional at all. The concept of "openness" encourages adopters to tell the child, at a very early stage, of its adopted state and to reinforce the message regularly. Contact, direct or indirect, may take place with some member or members of the birth family. The adopted person, once an adult, can search out the birth family and can enlist the help of various agencies to do this. Those who try to perfect the fiction by silence or pretence place the whole relationship with the adopted person at an awful risk.

The reality is that adoptive placements can, and usually do, work to the enormous satisfaction, exhaustion and joy that the biological production of children ought to. Very many adopters say that they could not have improved, by the conventional route, on what the adoptive process has given them.

Different adoption scenarios reflect the variety of things which adopters are seeking. The more conventional adoption setting involves an individual, or a couple, bringing up a young child as though it were their own child. These children are usually provided by Adoption Agencies (local authority Children's Services or Adoption Charities). Those bodies remain in place to offer post-adoption support to adopters, the child and birth families but in the main the adopters want to get on with their lives and to bring up their families in the usual way without continuing social worker involvement.

Step parent, or "partner of parent" adoption, is subtly different, the motivation being to replace only one of the birth parents. Sometimes the issue of curing the problems caused by the absent, replaced parent, is an important factor.

Foster carers often adopt a foster child. Sometimes the bond between foster child and carers transcends that of an ordinary foster care relationship; in other cases one wonders if the adoption isn't just a way of ridding the situation of the social care structure, for good or less good reasons.

The impulse for local authorities to have children placed for adoption, who would otherwise be in their long-term care, is a powerful one and successive government initiatives have encouraged it. This has been done in the teeth of a continuing decline in the numbers of adoptions generally.

In England in 1968 there were 25,000 adoptions; by 1996 the numbers were down to 6,000 and by 2003 the number was down to 4,500. The number has increased slightly over the past few years to 5,330 to year end 31-3-16.

The number of "looked after" children being adopted was, to March 2017, 4,350 (down from 4,960 the previous year). The number of children in care was, in 2017, 72,670, an increase of a couple of thousand from the previous year.

Governments of differing complexions, aghast at the increasing numbers of looked after children, have seen the adoption of children who have been removed from their birth parents as a highly desirable solution to the problem. Local authority Children's Services are, and have been for many years, the subject of both sticks and carrots designed to increase the numbers to which that solution was being applied. Decisions in the Court of Appeal and Supreme Court in 2013 gave a pause to what had become something of a "conveyor belt" for young children, where the prospect of return to birth families after their removal from them seemed far less than imminent.

Conventional wisdom is that this country is the only European country to permit opposed adoption. In fact almost all the countries of Europe have mechanisms, based on varying trigger factors, which permit adoption despite opposition from birth parents but they are, almost uniformly, hugely rarer than in the U.K., as are the numbers of adoptions generally.

Despite the relative enthusiasm for adoption in this jurisdiction, the power to order it only existed from the Adoption Act 1926. By the

1976 Adoption Act the regularisation and responsibility for advising the court on the subject was given to local authority Children's Services and, by the Adoption and Children Act 2002, the law relating to the subject was, supposedly, brought more into line with the Children Act 1989.

But for the adoption to be successful it must involve the right children and the right adopters.

CHAPTER TWO
THE ADOPTION & CHILDREN ACT 2002 WELFARE PRINCIPLE AND CHECKLIST

The 1976 Adoption Act contained its own fairly restricted "welfare test" in section 6 which provided that the court, in reaching any decision with respect to the adoption of a child, should "*have regard to all the circumstances, first consideration being given to the need to promote and safeguard the interests of the child throughout his childhood*".

Much was made academically of the difference between this test and the 1989 Children Act test set out in section 1(1) whereby the consideration given is "first" in adoption but "paramount" in other Children Act cases. In more recent practice, the courts were quite happy to give the interests of the child an almost identical priority and this welfare principle distinction eroded to virtually nothing as the Children Act mind set as to paramountcy became the norm.

So it seemed perfectly natural for the welfare test in the 2002 Adoption and Children Act to state that-

> "*The paramount consideration of the court or adoption agency must be the child's welfare throughout his life*"

More should have been made, but rarely was, of the other distinction between these two tests, namely the use at the end of the 1976 Act test of the words "*throughout his childhood*", as opposed to the more recent test's "*throughout his life*". In other words, we are not merely thinking of the here and now. Even in the case of a baby, the court should look, or should have been looking, at the impact of the order, not just for the whole of the next 18 years but far beyond. This concept chimes in with elements of the welfare checklist, in particular sections 1(3)(c) and (f) which look at how it will be to be an adopted person

Subsection 3 of section 1 copies the Children Act delay principle -

> "*The court or adoption agency must at all times bear in mind that, in general, any delay in coming to the decision is likely to prejudice the child's welfare.*"

Subsection 4 provides a checklist, which lists a number of other issues which the court or adoption agency must bear in mind (many of which are also lifted straight from the Children Act) namely:-

> *The court or adoption agency must have regard to the following matters (among others)—*
>
> *(a) the child's ascertainable wishes and feelings regarding the decision (considered in the light of the child's age and understanding),*
>
> *(b) the child's particular needs,*
>
> *(c) the likely effect on the child (throughout his life) of having ceased to be a member of the original family and become an adopted person,*
>
> *(d) the child's age, sex, background and any of the child's characteristics which the court or agency considers relevant,*
>
> *(e) any harm (within the meaning of the Children Act 1989 (c. 41)) which the child has suffered or is at risk of suffering,*
>
> *(f) the relationship which the child has with relatives, and with any other person in relation to whom the court or agency considers the relationship to be relevant, including—*
>
> *(i) the likelihood of any such relationship continuing and the value to the child of its doing so,*

(ii) the ability and willingness of any of the child's relatives, or of any such person, to provide the child with a secure environment in which the child can develop, and otherwise to meet the child's needs,

(iii) the wishes and feelings of any of the child's relatives, or of any such person, regarding the child.

This list is here set out as it was originally written but the Children & Social Work Act 2017, section 9, modified (f) so as to include, in the category of "any other person in relation to whom the court or agency considers the relationship to be relevant", "***any person who is a prospective adopter with whom the child is placed***".

This amendment followed a number of reported decisions where the issue of the relationship between a child, placed with an adoptive family for many months, or even longer, before the court finally adjudicated, and the adopters, appeared to have been given little or no consideration. These include-

Re P (A Child) [2015] EWCA Civ 777, in which King L.J. said that the court should pay great attention to the relationship which the child has with a foster carer, who had become a proposed adopter, with whom the child had lived virtually since birth.

Similarly, in **Re M'P-P (Children) [2015] EWCA Civ 584**, MacFarlane L.J. allowed an appeal against a special guardianship order in favour of an aunt in Belgium, who had only once even seen the children, rather than adoption by a foster carer who had looked after the children almost since their birth.

McFarlane L.J. observed that the 1st instance Judge makes "***no mention of the fact that they will no longer be cared for by the only primary carer they have known and will break the strong bond of attachment that they have with her*** (the foster carer/adopter)".

There was a similar outcome and reference to section 1(4)(f) in **Re W (A Child) [2016] EWCA Civ 793.**

ETHNICITY AND RELIGION

Section 1(5) of the 2002 Act used to make further reference to the child's background by saying that-

> "*In placing the child for adoption, the adoption agency must give due consideration to the child's religious persuasion, racial origin and cultural and linguistic background.*"

However, section 3 of the Children & Families Act 2014 removed that provision (in England, but not in Wales). The explanatory note to this part of the Act explains that this is to –

> "*Reduce delay by removing the explicit legal wording around a child's ethnicity so that black and minority ethnic children are not left waiting in care longer than necessary because local authorities are seeking a perfect or partial ethnic match;*"

What does the word "explicit" mean in this context?

Just how much attention or consideration should be given to these issues is a matter for conjecture. On the one hand, slavish "colour matching" might be objectionable and simplistic, but then again, clumsy trans-racial placements that tried to ignore true heritage have caused untold unhappiness.

Arguably, "background" does not just relate to colour or race. In Wales, for example, where the original provision remains, it is not unknown for those seeking adopters for a child born of Welsh speakers to seek Welsh speaking adopters.

While the "explicit legal wording around a child's ethnicity" is no longer a specific feature of the Act, those charged with finding adopters may still have to consider the religious background of the child. Would it be a hostage to fortune to place a child born of Muslim parents to be adopted by a Jewish family? In theory it should make no difference, but would it be wise?

And does subsection 4(c) of section 1 allow the court to ask itself what the likely effect (throughout his life) on the child would be of having ceased to be a member of the original family and becoming and adopted person in this particular family?

The former provision, (still, of course, current in Wales), refers to the "child's" religious persuasion. One might ask, when does a child acquire a religious persuasion?

In **Re C (A Child) [2012] EW MISC 15 CC** (which you will find in Family Law Week) a County Court Judge decided that a 10-year old girl, who wished to be baptised at the church which her father attended, should be allowed to do so despite the vehement opposition from her devout Jewish mother.

There is no mention in the 2002 Act of the 1976 Act's nod in the direction of respect for the religious persuasion of the parents, save for the "catch-all" provision in section 1 (4)(f)(iii) as to the parents' wishes and feelings generally. That Act's section 7 provided that "***An Adoption Agency in placing a child should have regard (so far as is practicable) to any wishes of a child's parents and guardians as to the religious upbringing of the child.***"

This wasn't taken very far by the courts; as early as 1962 in **Re G (An Infant) [1962] 2 QB 141** parents' wishes as to upbringing, although important, were not enough to prevent an otherwise appropriate placement. But section 1 (f)(iii) still provides that the wishes and feelings of the child's parents should be considered.

NO ORDER PRINCIPLE

There is now a "no order principle" akin to that in the Children Act. Section 1 (7) of the 2002 Act repeats the Children Act format but incorporates with it a provision that the court dealing with an adoption application must also consider its range of powers under the Children Act, saying –

> "***The court or adoption agency must always consider the whole range of powers available to it in the child's case (whether under this Act or the Children Act 1989); and the court must not make any order under this Act unless it considers that making the order would be better for the child than not doing so***"

A similar provision in the 1975 Children Act decimated for years the number of step parent and extended family adoptions by providing, in section 37, that before making an adoption order, the court should give consideration to whether it would be more appropriate to make a custodianship order (a now defunct precursor to a special guardianship order).

The 2002 Act's specific reference to the alternative powers of the court to make a Children Act order, should, arguably, be quite unnecessary. Adoption proceedings are "***any family proceedings in which a question arises with respect to the welfare of any child***" (s. 10 (1) Children Act) - allowing the court, of its own motion, to make s. 8 orders within such proceedings, if the court feels that such an order would be better. This definition also engages the court's power under section 14(6) of the Children Act to make a special guardianship order.

THE APPLICATION OF THE WELFARE PRINCIPLE AND CHECKLIST

To what court applications do all these welfare issues apply?

Subsection 7 makes them apply to a court-

> "*(a) coming to a decision in any proceedings where the orders that might be made by the court include an adoption order (or the revocation of such an order), a placement order (or the revocation of such an order) or an order under section 26 (or the revocation or variation of such an order),*
>
> *(b) coming to a decision about granting leave in respect of any action (other than the initiation of proceedings in any court) which may be taken by an adoption agency or individual under this Act,*"

Exactly why there should be a distinction, as far as the application of the whole of section 1 of the Act to leave applications is concerned, between applications in existing proceedings and those which "initiate" the case, may be hard to fathom. Fortunately the Court of Appeal in **Warwickshire County Council v M [2007] EWCA Civ 1084** dealt with this issue and rendered it innocuous.

CHAPTER THREE
THE ADOPTION APPLICATION

A. WHO CAN APPLY TO ADOPT?

Section 49 (1) of the 2002 Act sets out the helpful provision that an application to adopt can be by a couple or a single person and that if it is by a single person, the provisions of sections 50 and 51 apply.

ADOPTION BY A COUPLE

Both have to have habitually resided in the British Islands for at least 12 months (Section 49 (3)) and one of them has to be domiciled here (section 49(2)).

Both have to have attained 21 years unless one of the couple is the mother or father of the child and has attained 18 (but why would he or she be applying as, if it is a partner of a parent case, the birth parent doesn't have to apply?). Anyway, that is what section 50 says.

Much controversy raged in Parliament when the current Act was being debated, about the proposition that the word "couple" should include the unmarried and same sex couples. We all know that something virtually the same as "gay" couple adoption had been happening for years by the strategy of one of a same sex couple adopting and the other member then applying for what was then called a residence order and thereby sharing parental responsibility.

Ultimately section 144 was amended to include the provision that (in subsection 4) the word couple means "two people (whether of different sexes or the same sex) living as partners in an enduring family relationship".

There was also added a provision in subsection 5 of section 144 which prevents couples adopting where one person is the parent, grandparent, brother, sister, uncle or aunt of the other. This applies whether the relationship is of the whole or of the half blood, (subsection 6).

ADOPTION BY A SINGLE APPLICANT

Section 51 provides that the single adopter must be over 21 years of age and must be domiciled in a part of the British Islands, (section 49 (2)).

The current Act repeats the 1976 Act's provision that if a single applicant is married, then the applicant needs to give to the court a good reason why the application is not joint. The provision therefore allows such an application if the applicant is able to satisfy the court that the spouse "cannot be found", is permanently separated from the applicant or is incapacitated by ill-health from making the application jointly (section 51 (3)).

Similarly there is a repetition of the previous Act's provision preventing the adoption by one birth parent on his/her own (i.e. to the exclusion of the other parent) unless the other parent is dead or cannot be found, or, by virtue of section 28 of the Human Fertilisation and Embryology Act 1990, there is no other parent or there is "some other reason justifying it". (section 51 (4)). Such circumstances are, by their own nature, rare and based on unusual circumstances. An example can be found in-

Re A (A Child) [2015] EWFC 17, where Theis J dealt with a totally unopposed application for adoption by the birth "father", of a child born of a surrogacy agreement with an extended family member.

Section 35(1) Human Fertilisation and Embryology Act 2008 provides that where a married woman has a child by Artificial Insemination and her husband consents to that process, he is treated as the child's father.

The applicant was a single man and, as s. 54 of the 2008 Act provides that a parental order may only be sought by a couple, the surrogate "father" had to apply to adopt his own son, which he did, with support from the surrogate mother and her husband and from the local authority in its adoption report. He did not fall foul of the provisions of section 51(4) because of the presumption of parentage set out in section 35(1) of the 2008 Act. Had the surrogate mother and her partner not been married, presumably the biological father's adoption application would have had to have surmounted the "some other reason justifying it" hurdle.

B. PRELIMINARIES TO ADOPTION APPLICATIONS

RESIDENCE PERIODS WITH PROSPECTIVE ADOPTERS.

Section 42 of the 2002 Act deals with this issue. It ensures that a child can only be adopted if he or she has lived for a specified period of time with the prospective adopter – but the periods vary according to the type of adoption.

1. AGENCY PLACEMENTS

Where the child was placed by an adoption agency or in pursuance of an order of the High Court, (the section still says that) or where the applicant is a parent of the child, (that will rarely be the case) --- 10 weeks residence needs to have been completed before the application can be made (section 42(2)).

Hedley J in **EEC (The Local Authority) v SM [2011] 1 FLR 234** made it clear that the 10-week period could be spent outside the jurisdiction. He did, in that case, have to give approval under section 28 for the removal, and confirmed that this could only be done where the removal was temporary; (in that case he limited it to 6 months). In **Kent County Council v PA-K and IA (A Child) [2013] EWHC 578 (Fam)**

Mrs Justice Pauffley said that the fact that the child was placed in the USA for the time being (the family were in Florida) was no reason for the assessment of the placement not to take place, providing that the return to this country was anticipated and therefore habitual residence and domicile issues were unaffected.

2. PARTNER OF PARENT APPLICATIONS

If one of the applicants is the partner of a parent then the required residence period is 6 months (section 42(3)). For a helpful example as to how this might operate in practice see:-

Re X (A Child) [**2013**] **EWHC 689 Fam**; Theis J.

This was an application by a step-father to adopt his 15-year old step-daughter.

The Applicant was, it was found, domiciled in the British Islands, so that essential per-condition set out in section 51 of the 2002 Act was satisfied, although he worked principally in the Middle East, and returned only for short periods to his various homes in this country. The step-daughter was at a private boarding school and only spent occasional periods at the Applicant's home.

The oral evidence of the Applicant, as to how much time he had spent under the same roof as his step-daughter, was far less clear than his written evidence but the question was, had she had her home with the Applicant for at least 6 months prior to the application (s. 42(3) and did the local authority have an opportunity to see the child in her home with the Applicant?

Theis J found that –

1. In the 6 months prior to the notice of intention to adopt, the child had spent only a week with the Applicant;

2. “Home” can be widely interpreted, and does not include times when there has been merely email or social network communication;

3. The provisions of section 42(3) had not been met.

But by 2014, in a subsequent application, Theis J, in **Re X (A Child: Adoption No 2) [2014] EWHC 4813** was persuaded as to the 6 months’ residence period, despite boarding school issues and the fact that the step-daughter and father had still not clocked up 6 months’ worth of days together. Deciding that the residence period was not a matter of “bricks and mortar”, Theis J found that as the girl had spent her holidays from school residing with her step-father and mother, the condition was satisfied.

3. FOSTER CARER APPLICATIONS

If the applicants are local authority foster carers the required period is one year, (section 42(4)). This does not include applications by foster carers where the local authority Children’s Service formally match and approve the placement as an adoptive one. Such a placement, it is suggested, becomes an “Agency Placement” and falls under s. 42(2).

4. ANY OTHER APPLICATION

In any other case the period is 3 years (whether continuous or not) out of the 5 years preceding the application (section 42 (5)).

In 3 and 4 above, if the residence periods have not elapsed, section 42 (6) of the 2002 Act permits an application for leave to apply sooner. But in **Re IH (A Child) (Permission to Apply for Adoption) [2013] EWHC 1235** a High Court Judge at 1st instance refused permission to apply where the Applicant was clearly using adoption as a device to evade substantial Immigration irregularities and the “adoption” would be in name only and “altogether unreal”.

See also **Re A [2017] EWHC 1178 (Fam)** where Holman J adjourned an application to adopt the niece of an English woman, of Pakistani origin, where the application had been lodged on the day before the subject's eighteenth birthday (but there was some doubt as to whether the application had been issued with all the necessary accompanying documents). The main reason for the adjournment was the fact that notice of the application had not been served on the Home Office and the Secretary of State for the Home Department. That is an absolute requirement, said Holman J, when the outcome of the adoption application might have a bearing on the grant of British Citizenship.

There is, in the conclusion to section 42 (in subsection 7), a provision that in, any event, the court needs to be satisfied that the adoption agency, or local authority in the area where the applicants live if there is no agency involved, has had sufficient opportunity to see the child with the applicant(s) in their home together.

C. REPORTS AND NOTICES OF INTENTION TO ADOPT

The Agency which placed a child for adoption has to submit a report to the court on the suitability of applicants and any other matters relevant to the operation of section 1 (the welfare test) (Section 43). This report is referred to as the Annex A report. The matters to be set out in this report are detailed in Practice Direction 14C. The report covers a mass of details and information about the child, its birth, its birth parents and the prospective adopters.

In any case other than an agency placement, an applicant to adopt must give to the local authority **where he, she or they live**, a notice in writing of the intention to apply to adopt (S. 46). This triggers the preparation of an Annex A report.

The bold type is to emphasise that there is a difference between the need to serve notice only on the local authority where the applicants live, in the case of adoption, and the need to serve notice of intention to apply for a special guardianship order on the local authority where the applicants live, unless the child is "looked after", in which case it has to be served on the local authority doing the looking after (section 14 A (6) CA). There is no such distinction in adoption cases.

S. 144 confirms that "notice" means a notice in writing. There is no form prescribed by the Act or Regulations. It is suggested that the notice should give-

- the name and date of birth of the child;
- the names and dates of birth of parents;
- the addresses of parents;

A notice of intention to adopt is NOT necessary where the child has been placed for adoption by an adoption agency. In all other (non-Agency) cases a notice of intention to adopt is ESSENTIAL as without it an adoption order cannot be made, (section 44(2)) and will normally not be processed (but see Coventry v PGO below).

The application to adopt cannot be made until 3 months after the notice of intention to adopt has been given and no later than 2 years after it, (section 44(3)).

There may be scope for an element of flexibility as to what may amount to written notice.

In **Coventry v PGO [2011] EWCA Civ 729** the learned Judge was confronted by an urgent application to adopt by foster carers who were not approved by the local authority. They had given no notice of intention to adopt. The Judge decided to treat the defective application as a form of notice of intention to adopt, and provided an injunction to prevent the removal of the children. The decision to grant an injunction against the local authority to prevent removal was successfully appealed by the local authority, who had been about to place with approved adopters, (who, as a result of the appeal process, moved on to seek the placement of different children, much to the chagrin of the Court of Appeal.)

The purpose of the notice of intention to adopt is, as was the case in the 1976 Act and supporting regulations, to alert a local authority to a non-agency case and to trigger the preparation of a section 43 report.

Section 45 is the enabling provision which inserts the power to make regulations setting out what has to be in the local authority's report and paves the way for Practice Direction 14C. The section, in subsection 2, makes it clear that the regulations must provide that when reporting or considering a couple as adopters or prospective adopters "***proper regard is had to the need for stability and permanence in their relationship.***"

HEALTH REPORTS

In an agency placement, the adoption agency will have dealt with the issue of the health of the child and the adopters prior to approval of the idea of adoption for the child and of approval of the adopters by the agency and therefore there is no requirement for health reports on child or applicant(s).

There is also no requirement for these in a partner of parent application or an application by a birth parent.

The requirements for these reports, where they are necessary, are set out in the Annex to Practice Direction 14D. They are substantial and very detailed and include, as to the birth parent(s), "***a health history of each natural parent, so far as is possible***" and "***a full obstetric history of the mother***" then as to the child, a neo-natal history of the child and the results of a full medical examination.

Similarly detailed questions as to the health of the applicant(s) are set out in the latter part of the Annex.

There is a preamble to the Annex which explains that the report by the examining medical practitioner should cover the issues set out in the Annex "*as far as practicable*".

D. THE APPLICATION

The application to adopt a child who is habitually resident in the British Islands and is to be adopted in England and Wales is in Form A 58. There will need to be an application in respect of each child who is to be the subject of an application, rather than two or more children being dealt with on one form, as with a Children Act application.

Part 1 of the form deals with the details of the applicant(s) and includes, at the top of page 3, an opportunity to set out that this is a partner of parent application. There is no separate form for this particular type of application.

Part 2 provides for details about the child, including whether the placement was done by an adoption agency and whether this was as a result of one of a variety of possible orders.

Part 3 is where details of the child's birth parents are set out and allows for indicating whether the birth parent(s) consent to the application or whether the application follows the relinquishment of the child by the birth parent(s), (see later).

Part 4 allows the applicants to set out the names they wish the child to have after adoption. While many adopters retain the child's original first name or names (particularly where the child is not a very young baby), the adopters have the ultimate choice as to what the child will be called.

This section also provides for the annexing to the application of the health reports referred to above.

The court will require-

- An original and three copies of the application;
- An original or certified copy of the birth certificate of each child;
- If the consent of a birth parent is sought to be dispensed with, a statement setting out the facts relied on in the application to set aside that consent;
- A copy of any relevant order relating to the child or of any full, half or step sibling;
- Medical reports and 2 copies;
- Where a birth parent, or the spouse of an applicant, has died, a certificate of the death;
- A certificate of the marriage or Civil Partnership of the Applicants;
- A copy of any decree absolute of divorce or order dissolving or nullifying the civil partnership in respect of any applicant;
- If the applicant is a married person seeking to adopt as a single applicant, a statement setting out why;
- If the name of any applicant is different to the name on any evidence of marriage or civil partnership, any documentary evidence to explain the difference;
- "If available" –

- A copy of the photo page of the passport of each applicant;
- Any visa or page showing an entry stamp from Immigration Official;
- A copy of any driving licence showing the photograph of any applicant;

The court will also require the current fee applicable. In an agency placement, the agency will often pay the fee.

CHAPTER FOUR
APPROVAL OF APPLICANTS TO ADOPT

Never let it be said that becoming an approved adopter is easy or quick. But then perhaps it should be neither, as the end result of the process involves handing over, for life, someone else's child.

This process is governed by the Adoption Agencies Regulations 2005 ("the AAR") as amended by the Adoption Agencies (Miscellaneous Amendments) Regulations 2013.

Potential adopters who approach an adoption agency expressing an interest in adopting will be given a document called the "Adoption Passport" (which can be found on the First4Adoption web-site).

When the applicant(s) confirm that they wish to proceed, the agency should, according to the Department for Education Statutory Guidance, give an indication within 5 working days as to whether the agency is prepared to accept their "Registration of Interest". A face to face meeting or pre-arranged telephone call between agency and candidates informs the agency at this point. Only the clearest indicators of inappropriateness should result in refusal at this stage.

What then follows, over the next two months, is the "Pre-Assessment Process", where the agency carries out initial training as well as doing Police and health checks on the suitability of the applicant(s) and the taking up of references.

If the outcome of the Pre-Assessment stage is positive the Assessment stage begins, involving more intensive training and a full assessment of suitability to adopt. This stage will take some four months and will result in the social worker who carries out the assessment preparing a report for the Agency's Adoption Panel.

THE ADOPTION PANEL

The Adoption Panel is sort of committee, bringing together a number of professional participants (e.g. at least two experienced social workers, the medical adviser to the adoption agency, a member of the local authority council (if the agency is a local authority Children's Service) and at least three other "independent" members – (probably lay persons) of which at least two are to have had some personal experience of adoption).

The composition and activities of the Panel are governed by the AAR and are touched upon by a number of other Regulations and Government Guidances. Different local authorities and agencies have their own particular rules and protocols, within the general framework set out by the Adoption Agencies Regulations.

The Panel sits with a Chairperson and a minute taker and has access to a specialist lawyer from the Agency's legal team, who will not necessarily sit full time with the Panel but may be called upon when their meetings take place.

The social worker's report upon the prospective adopter(s) is presented to the Adoption Panel for it to consider making a recommendation as to suitability. Whenever the Panel is asked to make a recommendation as to suitability the applicant or applicants are invited to attend. The D.o.E Guidance suggests that–

> "*Panels can be stressful for prospective adopters and, as far as possible, should avoid being perceived as intimidating*"

There is no further guidance as to how this is achieved but great efforts are, we are told, made to make these events as welcoming and comfortable as is possible.

As with other processes of this and other Local Authority and Agency Panels, the outcome of their deliberation is not a decision but a recommendation to, if it be to a Children's Service, the "Agency Decision Maker", who, in the case of approval of potential adopters, makes the final decision.

One of the other, major duties of the Adoption Panel is to make recommendations as to the suitability of approved adopters to have placed with them for adoption a particular child or particular children. This process is called "matching" and, again, the recommendation as to the "match" goes to the Agency Decision Maker, for a final decision.

CHAPTER FIVE
STEP-PARENT, OR PARTNER OF PARENT ADOPTION

In days long gone, it was commonplace for a new spouse, (usually a new husband) to adopt the children of the other spouse by a former relationship. Superficially tidy though this may have been, it was often an excuse not to deal with some very important issues for the children concerned.

Those days are, in the main, gone but the strategy may still have appeal to some parents with care, when there is a new partner.

Occasionally it is the final "killer blow" at the end of a difficult contact issue, or where the absent parent, (usually the birth father) is so dangerous or destructive that the only solution is to, in law, erase him from the child's life.

This is as drastic a measure as any other adoption order, and the court will want to see genuinely compelling reasons for it.

But we should not dismiss the idea of step – parent adoption out of hand. It still has a place where it is really important for the child to be the "real" son or daughter of the non-parent partner. But we must expect the court, the social worker who, pursuant to section 43 of the ACA, has to file a report for the court, and any Children's Guardian who may be appointed, to look very carefully at the motives of the prospective adopter and the remaining birth parent "partner".

Adoption by a partner of a parent, under the current Act, does not need to be by both birth partner and new partner. Under all former Adoption Acts, because adoption orders, without fail, extinguished any and all pre-existing parental responsibility or "rights", both parent and step-parent had to apply to adopt. Section 46 (3) (b) now states that in a partner of a parent case, the parental responsibility of the parent in partnership is not affected by the order.

For a case giving guidance as to what issues are, and what may not, be appropriate for the court to bear in mind in a step-parent adoption case, see-

Re P (Step-Parent Adoption) [2014] EWCA Civ 1174

This case involved an English Applicant step-father whose Polish partner had two children, the first, a son, by a man with whom she had been in a very fleeting relationship, the second, a girl, by her former husband. Both fathers were Polish; the father of the son had little if any contact, the father of the daughter had seen her for the first few years of her life but not for the past nine years.

Neither father could even be traced, although service of the application to adopt was sent to the home of the daughter's paternal grandmother. At first instance it seems to have been thought that the unmarried father of the son needed to be served. In the end, this was impossible and he was never even traced.

There was a surprising lack of information, at both court levels, as to whether in Polish law the concept of parental responsibility existed, and if it did, whether either of these fathers had it. Both courts had to fall back on the assumption that similar provisions applied in Polish law as prevailed in the courts in England and Wales.

On that basis the first instance Judge decided that the father of the boy did not have parental responsibility but that the daughter's father did and that he needed to dispense with his consent before an adoption could be ordered.

The two children desperately wanted to be adopted, but the court, Guardian and the parents agreed that the court should either make orders in respect of both children or in respect of neither. To have one adopted and not the other was unthinkable.

The Judge at first instance was heavily influenced by the comments in the care case of **Re B (A Child) [2013] UKSC 33** about adoption being a "draconian" order, only to be made "as a last resort", etc. He decided that it was too draconian a step to cut the daughter off from her links with a paternal birth family and refused to make the order, and, consequently, to make either order.

In the Court of Appeal McFarlane L.J. stood all of that gently on its head, commenting that Re B was about a very different "cutting off" from the birth family, it was about a plan to have a child adopted by strangers to the absolute exclusion of the birth family, whereas this case was about the securing and enhancement of the only effective family that these children had. Adoption would equate with the children's strongly held wishes, and was manifestly in their interests. The actual orders were made that day, rather than for the case to be remitted.

For a salutary case about the need for honesty as to knowledge of the whereabouts of the birth father, should an applicant for a partner of parent adoption be tempted to be less than forthcoming, see-

Re J [2018] EWFC 8, which involved Cobb J dealing with the application of a birth father to appeal, in 2017, an adoption order made in May 2013, where the step-parent and the birth mother had been utterly dishonest – pretending that they had no idea as to the birth father's whereabouts. This was very far from the truth, they knew exactly where he was and how to contact him. The adoption order was set aside as a result of this "serious procedural irregularity".

CHAPTER SIX
ILLEGALITY

The thrust of the provisions in the 2002 Act as to illegality is to ensure, as far as is possible, that no-one should involve themselves in any arrangement that results in the placement of a child with prospective adopters unless this is carried out by or via an Adoption Agency.

There are criminal sanctions set out in sections 92 to 95 of the Act for making, agreeing to make, or receiving payments in connection with, adoption arrangements, (section 95), preparing reports in connection with a proposed adoption without being a person prescribed by regulations to do so (section 94), and for a number of other things set out in section 92 which are only to be permitted to be done by an adoption agency or pursuant to an order of the High Court. These are-

1. Asking a person other than an adoption agency to provide a child for adoption.

2. Asking someone other than an adoption agency to find adopters for a child.

3. Offering to find a child for adoption.

4. Offering a child for adoption to someone other than an adoption agency.

5. Handing a child over to someone other than an adoption agency with a view to adoption.

6. Receiving a child as in 5 above.

7. Entering into an agreement with any person for the adoption of a child or for the purpose of facilitating the adoption of a child where no adoption agency is acting on behalf of the child.

8. Initiating or taking part in negotiations of which the purpose is the conclusion of an agreement of a kind set out above.

9. Causing another person to take any of the steps set out above.

The offences set out in sections 92 and 95 are punishable, on summary conviction, by a term of imprisonment not exceeding 6 months or a fine not exceeding £10,000 or both (section 93 (5)).

Numbers 4, 5, 7, 8, and 9 above do not apply if the prospective adopters are parents, relatives, or guardians of the child or if the prospective adopter is the partner of a parent, (section 92(3 and 4)). But the practitioner should be extremely careful about this. It is not uncommon, in many cultures, for a person to refer, often innocently, to another as “my brother”, “my cousin”, or some other similar familial description when no such actual relationship exists.

Section 95 makes it an offence to make, receive, seek or arrange for the payment of money in connection with the adoption or consenting to the adoption of a child or the removal of the child from the jurisdiction for the purpose of adoption.

A glance at some of the unpleasant and mercenary things that go on in this business in some countries make it clear what mischief these sections seek to prevent, but it may, on occasions, not be too difficult to transgress without intending anything of the sort.

Less easy to do by accident is the act prescribed by section 123. Here it is forbidden, unless you are an Adoption Agency, to publish or distribute an advertisement or information that-

1. A parent has a child available for adoption,

2. Someone wants to adopt a child,

3. Someone other than an Adoption Agency is willing to facilitate an arrangement made illegal by section 92

4. Someone is prepared to receive a child illegally,

5. Someone is prepared to remove a child from the U.K. for the purposes of adoption.

Subsection 4 of section 123 makes it very specifically clear that publishing or distributing includes by electronic means and the internet is specifically included in that description.

The old law (section 24(2) Adoption Act 1976) absolute prohibition on the making of an order, or even on the hearing of the adoption application when a prohibited payment had been made is not reproduced in the 2002 Act. Any case, however, where the process is tainted by illegality of any kind, including, for example, the payment of money or the placement of a child for adoption by someone other than an Agency, will, or should, be referred for a High Court Judge to deal with. That does not, however, mean that the adoption order will not be made. The issue will be resolved by the application of the welfare principle and checklist.

Presumably the court will follow **Re G (Adoption: Illegal Placement) [1995] 1 FLR 403** and will continue to deal with an application which is tainted by illegality and will have the option to make or refuse the order.

There are far more frequent reported decisions on this sort of issue in the case law relating to surrogacy applications. The current Human Fertilisation and Embryology legislation (in particular the provisions of the Surrogacy Arrangements Act 1985) criminalise the commercialisation of surrogacy arrangements and section 54(8) of the Human Fertilisation & Embryology Act 2008 provides that a parental order shall not be made where money, apart from "expenses reasonably incurred" has changed hands between the parties "unless authorised by the court". That "authorisation" can be given by the court retrospectively.

A very convenient case exemplifying this and the comparison with adoption illegality is-

Re X & Y [2008] EWHC 3030 (Fam) where Hedley J said, as to in what circumstances it would be appropriate for a court to retrospectively authorise a payment that would otherwise prevent the making of a parental order –

> "*The statute affords no guidance as to the basis, however, of any such approval. It is clearly a policy decision that commercial surrogacy agreements should not be regarded as lawful; equally there is clearly recognition that sometimes there may be reasons to do so. It is difficult to see what reason Parliament might have in mind other than the welfare of the child under consideration. Given the permanent nature of the order under Section 30, it seems reasonable that the court should adopt the 'lifelong' perspective of welfare in the Adoption and Children Act 2002 rather than the 'minority' perspective of the Children Act 1989. On the other hand, given that there is a wholly valid public policy justification lying behind Section 30(7), welfare considerations cannot be paramount but, of course, are important. That approach accords with that adopted in the previous cases and also accords with the approach adopted towards the authorising of breaches of the adoption legislation. A particularly vivid example of this can be found in the judgment of Bracewell J in Re AW (Adoption Application) [1993] 1FLR 62. There the court was concerned in particular with serious (and indeed dishonest) breaches of Section 29 of the Adoption Act 1976 yet in the final striking of the balance between public policy considerations and the welfare of the child concerned the judge nevertheless made an interim adoption order.*"

CHAPTER SEVEN
PLACEMENT AND ADOPTION WITH PARENTAL CONSENT

It is hard to imagine a more difficult decision for a mother (and for a father, if one is involved,) than to resolve to hand over a child for adoption. For that reason, the 2002 Act, and the Adoption Agencies Regulations 2005, set out a formal process by which this decision is put into practice and regulated.

Section 18 of the 2002 Act provides that an Adoption Agency may only place a child for adoption if it has either a placement order, (as to that, see later chapters) or where section 19 of the Act applies, in other words, where the parent(s) consent. Throughout these provisions the words "parents" are followed by "or guardians" but for the sake of brevity this work will refer to "parents".

Section 52(6) of the 2002 Act explains that the word "parent" means a parent with parental responsibility. The section is headed "Parental etc consent". Subsection 6 does not say that this definition relates to the rest of the Act but it seems reasonable to conclude that in matters dealing with the giving of consent the word "parent" has the same meaning, although section 52 is actually focussed on the court dispensing with a parent's consent.

Section 19 of the 2002 Act explains that a parent can consent either to the placement with prospective adopters who the parent identifies in the consent, (Form A101 must be used) or may leave it to the Adoption Agency to choose the adopters, (Form A 100). Subsection 2 allows the parent who has identified adopters to also consent to placement with adopters of the agency's choosing if the child is removed from or returned by the adopters of the parent's choice (this will be on Form A102).

This consent route cannot be followed if there are ongoing care proceedings and if, subsequent to the consent being given, care or placement proceedings are issued, the consent route is, again, closed (section 19(3)).

Section 19 only refers to the placement of the child with adopters. It does not deal with the actual adoption process.

Section 20 deals with the parent consenting to the actual adoption of the child and confirms, in subsections 1 and 4, that the parent can give consent to placement and to the subsequent adoption at the same time. Form A103 provides for the consent to the actual adoption. Subsection 4 allows the parent to go further and to notify the agency that he or she does not wish to be informed of any application to adopt. There is no particular form for this notification but CAFCASS has a specific pro-forma for this purpose which can be accessed at Annex 5 of the **Good Practice Guidance for Adoption Agencies and Cafcass: Children Relinquished for Adoption.**

So, by one set of forms, the parent can indicate consent to placement for adoption, to the subsequent adoption order being made and to not being notified or involved in the process any further.

Obviously, the parent is entitled to be thoroughly informed and counselled before these steps are taken (AAR Regulation 21). The Agency will have given, or done its best to give, this counselling and information and the Guidance referred to above, together with Schedule 2 of the AAR, provides that CAFCASS will appoint a Reporting Officer who will visit the parent(s) to ensure that the consents being given are given freely and with full understanding.

This process, often called "relinquishment", does throw up one or two problems from time to time. The first of these deals with the time, after the birth of the child, when the process can start.

A. 6 WEEKS AFTER THE CHILD'S BIRTH

There are two confusing provisions in the 2002 Act regarding what can and cannot be consented to during the child's first 6 weeks.

The obvious "mischief" that these provisions seek to deal with is to ensure that mothers are not asked to give consent to massively important issues until they have had time to recover from the rigours of giving birth. If only the Act were clearer though.

Section 18(1) states-

> "*An adoption Agency may*
>
> *(a) place a child for adoption with prospective adopters, or*
>
> *(b) where it has placed a child with any persons (whether under this Part or not), leave the child with them as prospective adopters,*
>
> *but, except in the case of a child who is less than six weeks old, may only do so under section 19 or a placement order.*"

Section 52(3) states that-

> "*Any consent given by the mother to the making of an adoption order is ineffective if it is given less than 6 weeks after the child's birth.*"

There is no reference to whether a mother (let alone a father) can give consent to placement of the child for adoption. The question whether a mother can consent to placement before 6 weeks have elapsed from the birth and then has to wait until after that period to consent to the actual adoption was considered by Theis J in **Sandwell M.B.C. v GC & Others [2008] EWHC 2555 (Fam).**

In that case parents had accepted, because of what had happened to earlier children, that the child which the mother was about to deliver should be adopted. The signing and witnessing by a CAFCASS officer was done, as to both placement AND adoption, when the child was 4 weeks old (in error). The child had been placed with foster carers, with the parents' agreement under section 20 of the Children Act 1989.

When the adoption application came before Magistrates, the Legal Adviser noticed that the consent to adoption was premature and the case was adjourned. The CAFCASS officer revisited the parents, who, by this time had changed their minds and decided to refuse to consent and the matter was ultimately referred to Theis J.

The judgment in that case sets out with great clarity the illogicality in these provisions and the Judge suggests, following the 2002 Act's Statutory Guidance at paragraph 65, that the agency should not seek consent either to placement OR to adoption until the 6 weeks have elapsed.

As to what happens when the mother is adamant, as soon as the child is born, that she wishes for adoption - the 2002 Act's Statutory Guidance provides at Annex B a specimen 'written agreement' designed to comply with the requirement of r 35 AAR 2005, where a child is desired to be placed for adoption and is under six weeks old. That specimen agreement says "After the child is six weeks old the Agency will seek normal consent to the child being placed for adoption".

B. NON-DISCLOSURE OF THE IDENTITY OF FATHERS AND EXTENDED FAMILIES

Regulation 16 of the AAR 2005 obliges the adoption agency to obtain the information about the child's birth family that is specified in Part 3 of Schedule 1.

It is not entirely uncommon for birth mothers, or both birth parents, to refuse to give this information, particularly about birth fathers but also, not uncommonly, about anyone in the mother's family, sometimes for reasons of shame, cultural expectations, or both.

Part 19 of the Family Procedure Rules provides a vehicle by which the agency can seek the assistance of a High Court Judge of the Family Court to give a "*decision on a question which is unlikely to involve a substantial dispute of fact*', as happened **in M & N (Twins - Relinquished Babies - Parentage)** [2017] **EWFC 31.**

Here, the mother, a "mature, professional woman" who had been assessed by the local authority as perfectly capable of bringing up her older child, was adamant that she did not want anyone in the extended family to care for the twins she was expecting. Nor was she able, emotionally, physically or financially, to bring them up herself. She agreed to accommodation under section 20 of the Children Act but did not cooperate with many social work enquiries and it was not clear whether her family even knew about the birth of the twins, she having concealed her pregnancy until the last two weeks.

In this case, the limited information which the local authority obtained suggested that there were no realistic prospects for extended family carers and so Cobb J gave leave to the local authority NOT to make any further extended family enquiries.

There was a similar outcome, for different reasons, in **Re A (Relinquished Baby: Risk of Domestic Abuse)** [2018] **EWHC 1981 (Fam).**

Cobb J deals here again with this issue – mother does not wish father to be notified of the birth, saying that she is afraid of him and of repercussions from him.

In this case it turned out that when the local authority made enquiries, not only had the man been abusive to this mother but he was known to a number of other local authorities and Police Forces for domestic abuse and breach of orders, having a very poor history of criminality and mental instability.

Permission was given to proceed with the placement of the child, who mother wished to relinquish, without any notification of the man concerned.

But it does not always work out that way.

In **RA (Baby Relinquished for Adoption- Case Management) [2016] EWFC 25**, Cobb J adjourned an adoption application in the case of a baby born to and relinquished by his mother and placed with adopters. The maternal grandmother in Latvia, whose initial assessment by local assessors was positive, expressed a wish to bring the child up.

The local authority and the adopters asked for the adoption order to be made irrespective of the grandmother's wish but Cobb J refused, indicating that the court needed to have the full picture so that it could properly address the Adoption and Children Act welfare checklist.

The mother had expressed a very clear wish that her child be adopted here, not because she had any concerns about the standard of care her mother would give, but because of the advantages to her child of being brought up in this country.

The Judge considered the approach of Holman J in **Z County Council v R [2001] 1 FLR 365**, in which he had referred to the respect that should be given to a mother to make "*discrete, dignified and humane arrangements for the birth and subsequent adoption of their babies without their families knowing anything about it if the mother, for good reason, so wishes.*"

He then referred to **Re C v XYZ County Council [2008] 1 FLR 1294**, where Arden L.J. had said that the local authority should not simply accept what the mother say, should approach the issue critically and that the issue of whether the birth family should be informed was a matter of case by case judgment.

This case seems to be a clear example of the additional problems that can sometimes arise when it comes to parents from a foreign jurisdiction, living in England and Wales, who decide they wish to relinquish their babies. Another such case is-

Re JL & LO (Children) [2016] EWHC 440 (Fam)

This case concerned two children of two mothers, one from Estonia, one from Hungary, who had given birth in this country and had validly consented to placement for adoption here. Both local authorities were concerned that Brussels IIR might come into play and, effectively, applied for placement orders to protect the situation.

Estonia did not oppose the adoption here, but Hungary did.

Baker J decided-

1. Brussels IIR did not apply – this was a case entirely about adoption;

2. In a relinquishment case, Re B and the "nothing else will do" concept do not apply;

3. There is no jurisdiction for the court to entertain a placement order application – the mothers have relinquished and there is no care order or care threshold that has even been sought;

4. The court cannot use the Inherent Jurisdiction to cut across a statutory provision and direct a transfer to Hungary where Article 15 does not permit this.

As to the need, or otherwise, to inform the birth family, he said-

> *The wishes and feelings of the parents are likely to carry significant weight in the evaluation of the child's welfare. But they are not invariably decisive. As a result, the local authority cannot give any guarantee that it will keep the existence of the baby confidential. Each case will turn on its own facts. In some cases, an analysis of the circumstances will lead the local authority to conclude that it is unnecessary to inform the natural family, but in other cases the authority will decide that it must consult the extended family in order to carry out the necessary evaluation of the realistic options. Each case turns on its own facts, but the child's welfare will always be the paramount consideration".*

C. COMPETENCE TO CONSENT TO PLACEMENT

This issue was comprehensively addressed in-

S (Child as Parent - Adoption - Consent) [2017] EWHC 2729 **(Fam)**

The parent in this case was a young person below the age of 16 with significant learning difficulties. She had set her face firmly against having anything to do with her baby, who had been placed, from the hospital, with fostering to adopt carers.

The issue, which the local authority sought to have resolved, was whether the mother was capable of giving valid consent to adoption and, as the baby had been accommodated under Children Act section 20, the issue was extended to that of competence to consent to accommodation (despite, as Cobb J accepts, the section making no mention of the need to "consent" by a parent).

There was disagreement between the representatives of the local authority and the Guardian as to the extent of the issues of which, as to adoption, the child/parent needed to show understanding. The local authority suggested a more limited scope and Cobb J, although ultimately directing a further assessment of the mother's understanding of the issues, indicated that-

The test as to competence to agree to either course is that of "Gillick" competence. That means ability to-

a) Understand the nature and implications of the decision and the process of implementing that decision;

b) Understand the implications of not pursuing the decision;

c) Retain the information long enough for the decision-making process to take place;

d) Be of sufficient intelligence and maturity to weigh up the information and arrive at a decision;

e) Be able to communicate that decision.

Just because a child or young person lacks litigation competence in (for example) care or placement order proceedings, does not mean that she lacks subject matter competence in relation to consent to the adoption of the baby. It is therefore suggested that any capacity assessment, in a case where adoption of the child might conceivably become an issue, should involve an opinion as to the parent's capacity to consent, or otherwise, to adoption or placement for adoption, as well as capacity to instruct the lawyer generally.

As to consent to adoption the understanding must be that-

a) Your child will have new legal parents, and will no longer, in law, be your son or daughter;

b) Adoption is final, and non-reversible;

c) During the process, other people (including social workers from the adoption agency) will be making decisions for the child, including who can see the child, and with whom the child will live;

d) You may obtain legal advice if you wish before taking the decision;

e) The child will live with a different family forever; you will (probably) not be able to choose the adopters;

f) You will have no right to see your child or have contact with your child; it is highly likely that direct contact with your child will cease, and any indirect contact will be limited;

g) The child may later trace you, but contact will only be re-established if the child wants this;

h) There are generally two stages to adoption; the child being placed with another family for adoption, and being formally adopted;

i) For a limited period of time you may change your mind; once the child is placed for adoption, your right to change your mind is limited, and is lost when an adoption order is made.

The parent in this sort of case should have all possible assistance to achieve this understanding.

Cobb J also concluded, following the case of Re AO in 2016, that the fact of a mother having decided against trying to bring up her child in a way that was the opposite of abandonment could not lead to a care threshold. He said –

> "*That she has been clear in her wish to have nothing to do with T now does not represent her dereliction of parental responsibility, but an exercise of it.*"

D. PARENTAL RESPONSIBILITY AFTER RELINQUISHMENT

This is governed by section 25 of the 2002 Act. This provides that an agency that is authorised to place a child for adoption, both before and after the child is actually placed with adopters, has parental responsibility for the child (section 25(1)(a) and (2)).

Once the child is placed with adopters, they too have parental responsibility (section 25(3)).

But, importantly, both before placement with the adopters, and once the child is with the prospective adopters (until the actual adoption order is made, of course,) the parental responsibility which the agency has enables the agency to restrict the parental responsibility of the parents, guardians or prospective adopters of the child (section 25(4)). In other words, the agency will have the final say until the adoption order is made.

E. CHANGE OF MIND BY PARENT OR AGENCY

A. By parent

If consent to placement is withdrawn before the child is validly placed with approved adopters, the Agency has 7 days to decide whether to issue an application for a placement order (section 31(2) 2002 Act). This will almost certainly be combined with care proceedings. If none are issued after 7 days the child must be returned to the parent.

If the parent withdraws consent to placement, once the child has been placed with adopters, the Agency has 14 days to make the same decision (S. 32(2)),

However, section 32 (5) provides that if, before the request to return has been given, an application has, in fact, made for

- An adoption order,
- A special guardianship order,
- A Child Arrangements order seeking residence,
- Leave to apply for a CAO seeking residence or a special guardianship order,

and the application has not been disposed of, then there is no obligation to return the child unless the court dealing with the case so orders.

The situation is different, however, if the parent has given advance consent, not just to placement but to adoption under section 20 and wants to oppose the adoption application. In that case, the slightly tautological provisions of section 47 (2) (b) and subsection 3 suggest that a parent in that situation would need the leave of the court to oppose the application.

B. By the Adoption Agency

Section 35 of the 2002 Act provides that if the agency decides that the adopters should no longer have the child placed with them, they have to give a formal notice to that effect and 7 days later they can remove the child. There is no basis in the Act for an appeal to a court against this, but, the notice cannot be given once the adoption application has been issued – it is a matter for the court from then on.

But that procedure may not be enough to satisfy the Human Rights of the parties.

In **R (DL & ML) v London Borough of Newham May 2011** Mr Justice Charles heard a Human Rights Act application following the service of a section 35 notice and removal 7 days later.

In this case, a two and a half year-old child had been placed with approved adopters in April 2009. Only in June 2010 did the adopters in this case decide that they would proceed with the adoption application but they still did not actually apply. By August 2010, the local authority decided to bring the placement to an end, served their notice and collected the child 7 days later.

Charles J was critical of the local authority for not having discussions with the prospective adopters before issuing the notice, quashed their decision to remove as being in breach of the Article 8 rights of the adopters and the child, and said that, in an emergency, the authority should apply for an Emergency Protection Order or an Interim Care Order, so that a court could adjudicate upon the issue.

CHAPTER EIGHT
PLACEMENT ORDERS

This order marks the most extreme end of the ability of the State, represented by a Local Authority Children's Service, to erode, or, in fact, remove the right of parent and child to Family Life together.

A placement order, as set out in sections 21 to 29 of the 2002 Act, empowers a local authority to place the child concerned for adoption and compels it to seek, as its ultimate plan, only an adoptive placement. If and when it wishes to give up the search and settle for long term foster care, or some other non-adoptive alternative, it should apply to revoke its own placement order.

A. THE APPLICATION

The placement order can only be sought from the court in three scenarios-

1. Where the child is subject to a care order,

2. If the court is satisfied that the conditions set out in section 31(2) of the Children Act 1989 as to the making of a care order are satisfied. That refers to the care threshold. It is rare that a local authority does not ask for the care order to be made rather than to rely simply on the care threshold. The risk, if a care order is not obtained, is that if an adoptive placement is not found and the placement order is revoked, the local authority has no care order to fall back on and will have to apply all over again.

3. The child has no parent or guardian. Obviously, here, there is no way the child could ever be placed with consent.

A placement order (as with placement by agreement) gives the local authority parental responsibility; it is also given to the prospective adopters, once physical placement has happened. The type of parental responsibility which the local authority has enables it to restrict the parents' own use of their parental responsibility during the currency of the placement order prior to the actual adoption, (section 25, 2002 Act).

The placement order can only be made if the parent(s) consent to placement with any prospective adopters (this is likely to be where care proceedings have been commenced, otherwise the process under sections 19 and 20 will be used, unless the local authority considers that the consent may be withdrawn) or where the court dispenses with the parent's consent.

We return to section 52 of the 2002 Act on the subject of dispensing with the consent of any parent or parents of the child. Subsection 1 of that section provides that-

> *(1) The court cannot dispense with the consent of any parent or guardian of a child to the child being placed for adoption or to the making of an adoption order in respect of the child unless the court is satisfied that—*
>
> *(a) the parent or guardian cannot be found or is incapable of giving consent, or*
>
> *(b) the welfare of the child requires the consent to be dispensed with.*

The word "requires" has been the subject of much judicial emphasis and consideration and is the focal point of any contested placement order application. It involves the whole history of the child's journey into care, the prospects of reunification or placement within the extended family and the application, to all of this, of the 2002 Act's welfare checklist and the relevant sections of the Human Rights legislation.

In **Re P (Children)(Adoption: Parental Consent) [2008] EWCA Civ 535** a "parallel" approach to placement either by adopters or long term foster carers was approved by the Court of Appeal as a pragmatic and appropriate approach, in the case of children who would be very hard to place. But in **Re T (Placement Order) [2008] 1 FLR 1721,** where the children were clearly not in a condition where they could be adopted until therapy had proven successful, the Court of Appeal took the view that to make a placement order simply because, ideally, adoption would be the best outcome but where the children were at the time simply not yet adoptable, was premature and inappropriate.

Another successful appeal against a placement order happened in **Re H (Children) [2011] Court of Appeal 12th July 2011**. In this case there was no realistic prospect of the children going home to parents, because of lengthy drug abuse and criminality histories. The children were aged 6 and 8 and, at first instance, the Judge felt that adoption would be the right outcome. But the court had, according to the Court of Appeal, left too many unanswered questions about the attachments which the children had and their need for contact with birth parents and grand-parents. Those issues needed a better assessment before a placement order was appropriate.

Re A (Children) [2013] EWCA 1611 dealt with cross appeals by a local authority and the mother against placement orders made by the first instance judge, those orders having attached to them a number of "requirements" as to the attributes of adoptive parents. The trial judge had serious concerns about the important sibling relationships, both between the two children to be adopted and with the older three siblings, and about some behavioural issues the children suffered from.

The local authority contended that the "requirements" were conditions and that there was no basis in law for conditions to be attached to placement orders.

The Court of Appeal confirmed the "boundary" which exists between the making of a placement order and consideration of the specific placement. Only at the stage of the actual adoption application can the court pass a judgment about the actual adopters.

The judge's "requirements" overstepped the line that divides the responsibility of the court and the responsibility of the agency charged with finding a placement.

If there were so many reservations about the potential adoptive placement could it really be said that adoption was in the children's welfare and that "nothing else will do" when it comes to dispensing with parental consent?

In **Re B (A Child) [2013] UKSC 33** the Supreme Court took the opportunity to review a case where the child had been removed at birth because of mother's grossly dysfunctional history and personality and father's equally serious history of criminality and antisocial behaviour. The parents had, despite these problems, behaved well at contact for over two years and had shown themselves devoted to the child. The local authority's care and placement order case was based on their assertion that there was no prospect of this couple ever being able to safely parent or to work with a local authority.

In judgments which dealt with a number of very fundamental issues, including the interface between the test of "balance of probabilities" as to finding of past facts and "real possibility" as to the degree of likelihood to find that a child was "likely to suffer harm if an order is not made", the court looked at the word "requires" in section 52 of the Act and made it clear that it is not enough that it would simply be "better" for the child to go down the adoption road, a far more stringent test needed to be applied.

The views of the Supreme Court Judges in Re B were summarised and quoted with much approval by the then President in **Re B-S (Children)**

[2013] EWCA Civ 1146, where he lists a number of descriptions given, within those judgments, of a care plan for placement for adoption as-

> *"a very extreme thing, a last resort", only to be made where "nothing else will do", where "no other course [is] possible in [the child's] interests", they are "the most extreme option", a "last resort – when all else fails", to be made "only in exceptional circumstances and where motivated by overriding requirements pertaining to the child's welfare, in short where nothing else will do".*

In a decision shortly before Re B-S, MacFarlane L.J. had, in **Re G (A Child) [2013] EWCA Civ 1146,** criticised social worker's and Guardians' reports, as well as court judgments, which did not, in the setting out the case for a placement order, provide a clear "balancing exercise". By that he meant that it is not appropriate to examine, starting from the least invasive of the parents' rights, each of the options for the child's future care and, if all others are found wanting, to simply stop at the placement order as a solution without subjecting that to the same degree of critical analysis. He described that defective process as "linear".

B. THE EFFECT OF THE PLACEMENT ORDER

Just as with formal relinquishment of the child, section 25(1) and (2) of the 2002 Act provides that once a placement order is made the Adoption Agency has a form of parental responsibility that can restrict the operation of the parental responsibility which any parent or guardian has and of that of the prospective adopters once the child has been placed.

A placement order continues until it is revoked, or the child is adopted, or the child reaches 18, or marries before then (section 21 (4).

Once there is authority to place by consent or by a placement order, a parent or guardian may not apply for a child arrangements order seeking residence and no-one may apply for a special guardianship order unless, during the application to adopt, the court gives leave to do so (Section 28 (1) and section 29 (4) and (5)).

Once there is authority to place following relinquishment or a placement order, no-one may, without leave of the court or the written consent of each parent, change the child's surname or take the child out of the country unless the removal is for a period of less than one month by a person who provides the child's home (section 28 (2) and (3).

A placement order does not extinguish a care order - it simply causes the care order to have no effect while the placement order is in effect (section 29 (1)). The placement order WILL however extinguish any section 8 order or supervision order (Section 29(2)).

No specific issues, prohibited steps, supervision or child assessment orders can be applied for while a placement order is in force (Section 29(3)).

C. THE TIMING OF THE PLACEMENT ORDER APPLICATION

Section 22 of the 2002 Act provides that, where a child is looked after (in care, accommodated, etc) or has no parents or guardians AND the local authority is satisfied that the child ought to be placed for adoption, an application for a placement order must be made. The implication, it is suggested, is that the placement order application should be made promptly.

The interaction of the process by which the local authority makes itself ready to issue an application for a placement order and the 26-week timetable, introduced into section 32 of the Children Act 1989 by the

Children and Families Act 2014 section 14, can cause the local authority massive headaches.

A Looked After Children Review will have recommended the outcome. The social worker will have to complete a wide-ranging report on the child and the history of the case (called the "Child Permanence Report"). Adoption Agencies Regulations – Reg 17 (1) provides for this and sets out what the report should contain. That report, and health reports on the child and, if possible, the parents, will go to the Authority's "Agency Decision Maker", a senior Children's Service Manager, who will actually decide whether the plan for adoption is appropriate to the child. That process will take many weeks and can eat up massive proportions of the 18 or so weeks after the issue of proceedings which are generally allowed before the local authority has to file its final evidence, thanks to the rigorous demands of the 26-week timetable.

Long before 26 weeks became the target, the need to move cases along and the consequent temptation to issue any placement application at the last minute led to the case of **Re PB (Placement Order) [2006] EWCA Civ 1016**, in which the Court of Appeal refused an appeal by a mother in a case where a placement order application had been lodged during the several days of final hearing of a care case. Despite protests that the mother's legal team had, effectively, no notice of the application, the trial judge indicated that he would hear the placement application as well and found for the local authority.

The Court of Appeal held that, as the mother's legal team knew that an application for a placement order was likely, knew what the application would be and that the application turned on the same background evidence, the trial judge was not wrong to have proceeded.

Shortly after this, the Family Justice Council Guidance on Linked Care and Placement Order Applications was issued, which recommended, among many other issues, that –

> *"it is to be hoped that the IRH will be fixed so that any application can be issued at least 7 days earlier so that all parties have a proper opportunity of considering their position prior to the advocates meeting and hearing."*

This, of course, was long before the 26-week timetable was introduced, as at least an aim, in all care and placement cases so it is not at all guaranteed that the recommendation, or "hope", of the Family Justice Council will prevail over the drive to achieve this statutory target. It is as well to anticipate that a placement order application will emerge at what may appear to be the "last minute" in the care case, to have advised the parent well in advance and to ensure legal aid cover for that aspect of the case.

The case of **S-F (A Child)** [**2017**] **EWCA Civ 964** involved the Court of Appeal commenting, obiter, that it is poor practice not to include the permanence report and the record of the Agency Decision Maker's decision in the court bundle, although in that case the absence of these did not pave the way to a successful appeal.

D. THE PLACEMENT ORDER ITSELF

A properly drafted order will involve either a recital that the parent(s) consented to the order or a specific order by the Family Court that the parent(s)' consent was dispensed with. It will then go on to provide that a placement order is made in favour of the Applicant Local Authority.

At times, the parent can see that the placement order is bound to be made, because the case for it is overwhelming. It is not uncommon for the representative of a parent in such a situation to be instructed to indicate that the parent "does not consent to but does not oppose" the making of a placement order. That will result in the Family Court having to find and set out reasons for the dispensing with the parent's consent, and, apart for the discomfort to the parent of having to listen to that, this, in itself. may not be a significant problem.

But the order itself will be one of the documents that those adopted persons who wish, as adults, to have access to their records, will be able to see. If the birth parent can possibly bring herself (or himself) to actually consent to the order, the adopted person will see that the process had the consent of the birth parent and the existence of this "blessing" may be an important and positive piece of information to find.

The myth that "I fought for you", as well as misleading, in the case of the order which was nether consented to nor opposed, does not give the positive message that folklore in some quarters might attribute to it.

E. PLACEMENT TIMESCALES

Anyone considering that placement orders, or their predecessors under the 1976 Act, "Freeing orders", provide some automatic route to an adoptive panacea needs to read the judgment of Jackson J in **A & S v Lancashire County Council [2012] EWHC 1689 (Fam)**. In that case two brothers, one aged 16, the other aged 14, took proceedings against the local authority for negligence, breach of their Human Rights and breach of statutory duty. The boys had been removed from, or abandoned, by their parents as a 2-year old and a baby of a few months and, eventually, were made the subject of orders freeing them for adoption (under the 1976 Act): but adopters were never found. In the ensuing 11 years, the older boy had 77 different placements, the younger, 96. They were not treated with uniform kindness in all of those placements.

The local authority had never taken any steps to seek the discharge of the freeing orders and so the boys remained in a sort of statutory limbo, once home finding had been abandoned.

The judgment is fiercely critical of the local authority and had the result that Children's Services across the jurisdiction were directed by Government, to check how many children remained the subject of freeing or placement orders when there was no realistic prospect of adoptive placements being found and no ongoing search for such placements. There were thousands of such children. The direction involved these Services to make applications to get the children back into the care system.

One other result of this case, and the consequent scrutiny of the numbers of children in that sad category, was that, as a matter of good practice, the placement order, or the local authority's care plan, (or, ideally, both,) should contain a recital as to how long the search for adopters will be maintained and that, in the event of the search being fruitless at the end of that period, the local authority will seek a discharge of the placement order. This will return the child to the care system with the usual care order checks and balances and, subject to section 34(4) of the Children Act 1989, to the obligation on the local authority to afford some form of contact with the birth parents.

As a general rule, the period of the search tends to be 6 to 12 months.

It is suggested that even in the case of a healthy baby, who ought to be easy to place, such a recital would be good practice.

CHAPTER NINE
REVOCATION OF PLACEMENT ORDERS AND OPPOSING ADOPTION

There are three places in the 2002 Act where the ability to obtain leave to do things depends on persuading the court that there has been a "change in circumstances" or, in one case, a "significant change in circumstances". The first two are about attempts to get the child back when a placement order has been made, namely –

1. Section 24(3) – in an application for leave to apply to revoke a placement order,

2. Section 47(5) – in an application for leave to oppose an adoption order.

The third leave example which depends on a change in circumstances relates to special guardianship and is found in section 115 of the 2002 Act.

A. LEAVE TO APPLY –

- TO REVOKE THE PLACEMENT ORDER

When it comes to trying to reverse the process through which the child subject to a placement order is going, timing is everything. Section 24(2) makes it clear that once the child has been placed with adopters, only the local authority or the child can apply for leave to revoke – no-one else can. Hence-

> "*an application to revoke may not be made by a person other than the child or the local authority…unless –*

(a) the court has given leave to apply , and

(b) the child is not placed for adoption by the authority)."

So the parent wishing to revoke the order can only apply to do that up until the time when the child is placed with adopters. In fact it is not just the birth parent who can apply – section 24 (1) provides that-

> "*The court may revoke a placement order on the application of any person*".

The important caveat to this is that, pursuant to subsection (3) of section 24 –

> "*The court cannot give leave under subsection 2(a) unless it is satisfied that there has been a change in circumstances since the order was made*".

Subsection 5 of section 24 prevents a local authority which has a placement order from actually placing the child with adopters once a person has surmounted the leave hurdle and has made the actual application to revoke. The actual wording is that-

> "*Where—*
>
> *(a) an application for the revocation of a placement order has been made and has not been disposed of, and*
>
> *(b) the child is not placed for adoption by the authority,*
>
> *the child may not without the court's leave be placed for adoption under the order.*"

But, technically, the local authority with the placement order can still go ahead and place the child when only a leave application has been lodged – but it would be a brave local authority that did that, unless there were very exceptional circumstances, as cases set out later will show.

- TO OPPOSE THE ADOPTION APPLICATION

Section 47 of the 2002 Act is more convoluted. (We have already seen the slightly confusing terminology in subsections 2(b) and 3 as to the opposition of a parent who has given consent under section 20 but wishes to oppose the adoption).

Section 47 covers the conditions which have to prevail, in different situations, before an adoption order can be made. The second such situation is where an adoption order is applied for after a placement order has been made. Subsection 4 describes this as where –

> "*the child has been placed for adoption by an adoption agency with the prospective adopters in whose favour the order is proposed to be made,*
>
> *(b) either—*
>
> *(i) the child was placed for adoption with the consent of each parent or guardian and the consent of the mother was given when the child was at least six weeks old, or*
>
> *(ii) the child was placed for adoption under a placement order, and*
>
> *(c) no parent or guardian opposes the making of the adoption order.*"

This is then followed by subsection 5 –

> *(5) A parent or guardian may not oppose the making of an adoption order under the second condition without the court's leave*"

And by subsection 7 –

> *"(7) The court cannot give leave under subsection (3) or (5) unless satisfied that there has been a change in circumstances since the consent of the parent or guardian was given or, as the case may be, the placement order was made."*

So –

i. the person seeking the revocation of the placement order where the child has not been placed, or

ii. the parent or guardian (the category of prospective applicant is more restrictive under the leave to oppose provisions) seeking to oppose the adoption AFTER the child has been placed,

all need to establish that there has been a "change in circumstances since the order was made".

Interestingly, the third "change in circumstances" example, which refers to applications to discharge a special guardianship order, prefaces the words "change in circumstances" with the word "significant". The case of **Re G [2010] EWCA Civ 300** confirms that the word "significant" adds absolutely nothing to the expression.

Case law certainly suggests that an "insignificant" change in circumstances will, in the context of seeking leave to revoke a placement order or to oppose adoption, get the applicant nowhere at all.

B. THE TEST OF CHANGE IN CIRCUMSTANCES

1. LEAVE TO APPLY TO REVOKE PLACEMENT ORDERS

In **Warwickshire County Council v M [2007] EWCA Civ 1047** the first instance judge had found a change in circumstances where a mother was able to set out wide-ranging improvements in her life. Her use of crack cocaine had ceased for over two years and cannabis use had ceased for nine months. The dangerous and mentally ill father of one of the children had been deported and had then died; the mother's home was being well looked after, she had ceased all "romantic associations", undertaken necessary health care steps which she had previously neglected and had held down employment.

The application for leave had been precipitated, it was found, by disclosure to the mother that adopters had been found, and a "goodbye" contact had taken place. The two children, one of whom had some disabilities, were always going to be hard to place.

The trial Judge had considered a provision in section 1 (7)(a) of the 2002 Act, which provides that section 1 of the Act (which contains the paramountcy principle as well as the Act's welfare checklist) does not apply to a leave application which "initiates" proceedings. He interpreted this as meaning that once a change in circumstances has been found to exist, in a leave to revoke application, (which will be free-standing, as opposed to a leave to oppose an actual adoption application, where there are already other proceedings underway, namely the adoption application), there is no scope to do anything but to grant the leave.

The Court of Appeal agreed with the trial judge as to the background facts amounting to a change in circumstances but then went on to disagree with his interpretation of the consequences of section 1(7)(a). Wilson L.J. agreed with the trial judge that, as in any leave application, there was a need to find that the substantive application, would have a "*real, (as opposed to a fanciful) prospect of persuading the court to revoke the placement order)*". But the substantive application, he said, was not one requiring leave and so deciding that case very clearly involved consideration of the welfare checklist and paramountcy principle. Accordingly, any assessment of the prospects of success would clearly require reference to the interests of the children.

So the fact that hard to place children had been found adopters and had gone through a goodbye contact was entirely relevant to the exercise of judicial discretion to grant leave. The judgment then goes further and finds that, despite the very considerable changes in the mother's circumstances, the risk of losing an adoptive placement for hard to place children such as these was just too great and that, therefore, the discretion to give leave should not have been exercised.

In that case Warwickshire earned praise for their decision, on learning that mother was seeking leave to apply for a discharge, not to place the children with the adopters who were found and matched. It must have been tempting though.

In **Re F [2008] EWCA Civ 439** the Court confirmed, as the statute sets out very clearly, that where the local authority forged on and placed there was absolutely nothing the Court could do but to deprecate the local authority's actions.

A birth father, who had not played a part in the care proceedings, sought to become involved in the case when he learned that the child was about to be placed with adopters. He sought leave to apply to revoke but in the 10 days that his application sat in the Court office awaiting listing, the local authority went ahead and placed the children. At 1st instance and in the Court of Appeal, the Courts confirmed their helplessness – but the Court of Appeal indicated that the social workers were ill-trained and ill-managed and the arrogance of the Agency's behaviour was "***the most shocking aspect***". The Court of Appeal suggested that, in future, the parent's solicitor in such a situation should invite the local authority to undertake not to place and if that invitation was not immediately taken up, they should make an ex parte application to the court for an injunction ordering that placement should not go ahead pending the outcome of the leave application.

In **R (On the Application of EL) v Essex County Council [2017] EWHC 1041 (Admin)** we find Charles J dealing with an application in the Administrative Court to quash the decision to place a 6-year old child with adopters.

The mother had failed in her application for leave to appeal the making of the placement order and was in the process of seeking leave to apply to revoke it (her application had been lodged but she had not paid the fee,) when the local authority accelerated the placement plan.

Charles J found that the acceleration appeared to be because the local authority was concerned that mother may get her leave and that this would, of course, as a result of section 24(5) of the ACA, make it impossible to place the child once her substantive application was lodged, unless the court gave leave.

As it was, instead of accelerating the process, the Local Authority should have paused, awaited the outcome of the leave application or, if speed was necessary, made an application to the court for leave to proceed with the placement under section 24(5).

In finding this, Charles J referred to the Statutory Guidance on Adoption, which says, in paragraph 5.2-

> *"It is not however appropriate for a local authority to proceed with the placement when it is aware of the application for leave, and an attempt to do so in order to frustrate the birth parents' application could be challenged in court by an application for judicial review. In* **Re F (Placement Order)** *[2008] EWCA Civ 439 the Court of Appeal stated that the appropriate course of action in such a case would be for the birth parents to request the local authority to delay placement until the application could be heard. If such a delay is likely to be prejudicial to the child's welfare, for example if introductions have already started, the local authority should then apply to the court as quickly as possible for permission to place the child, under section 24(5) of the Act."*

Charles J found the placement unfair and quashed it.

As to certainty of the exact moment when a child is placed, in **Coventry City Council v PGO and FEO [2011] EWCA Civ 729** Wilson LJ clarified that a child is not placed until he actually begins to live with his adopters, or, when he is already living with them i.e. as foster carers, when the adoption agency confirms their status as adopters.

In **R (A Child - Whether to revoke Placement Order)** [2017] **EWHC 2924 (Fam)** Hayden J dealt with a leave application where the alleged change in circumstances involved the possibility that the current foster carer of the 3-year old child might be prepared to care for the child in the long term as a special guardian. The Judge refused to accept that the suggested basis for leave actually amounted to a change in circumstances – it was simply too speculative and was "misconceived".

2. LEAVE TO OPPOSE ADOPTION APPLICATION CASES

The first example, chronologically, of an appeal in relation to one of these leave applications was in **Re P (A Child)(Adoption Order: Leave to Oppose Making of Adoption Order)** [2007] **2 FLR 1069.** Here the Court of Appeal considered the first instance refusal of leave to oppose the adoption of children who had been removed by way of care and then placement order proceedings

The birth parents in Re P had missed the chance to apply to revoke the placement order as the child had been quite promptly placed with adopters. They argued that their circumstances had changed and that they should have leave to oppose the adoption application because-

1. Father was now having contact to his child by a previous relationship – there having been an issue of domestic violence in that relationship,

2. The parents had had another child, had successfully undergone residential assessment and were back in the community bringing up that child.

The 1st instance judge decided that these issues did not amount to a change in circumstances but that in any event the provisions of section 1 (7) ACA applied, namely that the court had to give paramountcy to the child's welfare in "*coming to a decision relating to the adoption of a child*".

As we have seen, section 1(7)(b) explains that this test covers-

> "*coming to a decision about granting leave in respect of any action (other than the initiation of proceedings in any court) which may be taken by an adoption agency or individuals under this Act*".

The Judge then decided that, even if the fact did amount to a change of circumstances, the application would fail on the paramountcy of the child's welfare basis.

There was just a hint of a raised judicial eyebrow in the Court of Appeal at the proposition that the facts did not amount to a change of circumstances but the court agreed as to the paramountcy argument and refused the parents' appeal.

As to what might amount to the sort of change in circumstances that might suffice, Wall L.J. said that it must –

> "*.. be of a nature and degree sufficient, on the facts of the particular case, to open the door to the exercise of the judicial discretion*"

In **Re W (A Child) [2010] EWCA Civ 1535** there had been a mistake in the local authority's documentation as to the mother's home address. When, after a placement order, the child was placed with adopters and they duly applied to adopt, the notice from the court never reached the mother.

2 years later the mother learned of the fact of the adoption order and applied to have it set aside. A High Court Judge (Holman J) granted the order setting the adoption aside. The mother also sought leave to join in and oppose the new application to adopt, arguing that her attaining freedom from drug dependency was a change in circumstances which entitled her to leave to oppose. The child was, by this time, 5 years old.

The Court of Appeal upheld the adopters' appeal against the grant of leave, saying that although there clearly had been a change in circumstances, the grant of leave depended on whether the giving of leave was in the child's best interests and that in the instant case, in view of the passage of time during which the child had, to all intents, been adopted, there were "*very powerful current imperatives in favour of adoption*".

However, in **Re B-S (Children) [2013] EWCA Civ 1146** the President said that the comment, in Re W, by Thorpe LJ that leave to oppose would only be given in "*exceptionally rare circumstances*" went too far.

In **Re W (A Child); Re H (Children) [2013] EWCA Civ 1177** we find the Court of Appeal dealing with two appeals against first instance refusals to permit joinder and opposition to the adoption application, under s 47(5).

In both cases the original court had accepted that there had been a change in circumstances but in both the reason for permission nevertheless having been refused was that the children concerned had been placed with adopters and that their welfare would not be enhanced by "unscrambling" (a quote from the 1st instance judgment in Re W) these arrangements;

The judgment of the President indicated clearly that this is not the test to apply.

Both 1st instance judgments were given well before Re B-S,

The President makes allowances for this, but as there was no analysis of the "*solidity*" of the prospects of success (and in pre-B-S cases there is no need for the court to have used the expression "solid" or "solidity" as long as the issue is covered) the appeals were allowed.

Re L (Leave to Oppose making of Adoption Order) [2013] EWCA Civ 1481 involves a mother's appeal against refusal at first instance to give her leave to join in and oppose the adoption application, where her circumstances had improved, (partly by the passage of time – she having been 15 when the child was born).

She had had her final contact in February 2012, the child, now 4, was placed with adopters the following month but the adopters, having applied to adopt in July 2012, separated in October that year. The child remained with the prospective adopter father, and there was some doubt as to whether, in any event, an adoption order would be made in his favour.

The first instance judge separated out the issues of –

a. Whether there had been a "change in circumstances";

b. The question mark over the adoptive placement.

Black L.J., accepting that the original decision was pre- Re G (the "linear" argument case), said of the judge –

> "*... he appears to have been looking for quite a high degree of present certainty in this regard, speaking for instance of M being unable currently to "satisfy" the court of her abilities. The degree to which a court needs to be confident about a parent's abilities at the section 47(5) stage is likely to vary, in my view, depending on the other circumstances of the case and I say a little more about this in the final paragraph of this judgment. Where the other option under consideration also has significant uncertainties, a lesser degree of confidence*

> *may sometimes justify the granting of leave and it seems to me that that was so here."*

But she went on to add, in a more general vein –

> *Where, for instance, a child has been placed with adopters for a protracted period, is well settled, and remembers nothing else, a court may well take the view that there has to be a degree of confidence about the parent's ability to provide a suitable home for the child before it can even contemplate assessing the parent's prospects as solid. And the cases show that the overall circumstances of the case may be such that the court may decide not to grant leave even where there is some confidence in the parent.* Re B-S *was an example of a mother who had achieved "an astonishing change of circumstances" (*Re B-S, *§3) but did not get leave to oppose adoption because of the situation of the children.*

The mother's appeal was upheld and leave to oppose was given, the Court of Appeal finding that insufficient weight was given to the question marks over the adoptive placement.

In **Re D (Leave to Oppose Making of Adoption Order)** [2013] **EWCA Civ 1480** a mother, whose improvements in circumstances were not considered by a first instance judge, to be sufficient, appealed against the refusal of section 47(5) leave. The Judge had weighed in the balance a very settled adoptive placement, where the child, now 3 years old, had been for 9 months at the original hearing.

On appeal Black L.J. found that, in another pre-Re G and B-S decision at 1st instance, while the judge had not used the word "solidity" to describe what was lacking in the mother's case, – the right test had been used and the refusal was correct.

Re LG (A Child) [2015] **EWFC52** dealt with a young couple, whose termination of an earlier pregnancy had brought huge shame to the father's family, were simply too scared to tell them about the child that was born a year or so later.

Care proceedings were commenced in March 2014 and concluded in August, neither parent having advanced any potential kinship carers. The baby was placed with adopters and the father eventually told his family in December that year. They immediately came forward as potential carers and were found suitable. The local authority and Guardian ultimately both supported the father's leave application.

Baker J, hearing that the local authority and Guardian would have considered the grandfather's family as potential carers, and that they would have probably placed the child with his family rather than to have sought or supported placement for adoption, indicated that there had been a change in circumstances and that the chance of opposing the adoption application had more than "solidity".

Re P (A Child) [2015] EWCA Civ 777. Here the mother had a history of violent anger outburst and an inability to work with those in authority. Her fifth child was placed with foster carers, from 3 days old and they had been approved and matched to adopt him. Mother's application for leave to join in the adoption application and oppose the adoption had been refused by a circuit judge, despite mother having had her 6th child and beginning to show signs of a positive response to a regime of therapy. There were proposals to return the 6th child, (still a few months old) to her.

King L.J., refusing the appeal, said that the welfare test issue of consideration of the effect on the child of ceasing to be a member of its original family and becoming an adopted child had to be balanced against the other factor of the relationship which the child has with relatives and other relevant persons – so the particular relationship which the child has with a foster carer from birth is not to be ignored and, in fact, is particularly significant in that context.

CHAPTER TEN
THE ADOPTION ORDER

The consequences that flow from the making of an adoption order are set out in section 46 of the 2002 Act. They are perhaps obvious, in that-

1. The adopter(s) obtain parental responsibility,

2. The order extinguishes -

   i. The parental responsibility of anyone who previously had it,

   ii. Any pre-existing Children Act 1989 order, or similar Scottish or Northern Ireland order

   iii. Any duty to pay maintenance or periodical payments.

3. The order does not extinguish maintenance arrears up to the date of the order nor a duty arising in a trust or one expressed to continue after adoption. See **Staffordshire C.C. v B [1998] 2 FLR 431** for a case on trusts and adoption.

Cases such as Staffordshire County Council v B make it absolutely vital that those contemplating adoption for a child, or placement for adoption, remember to check on the financial consequences of the order they seek. Wealth lurks in the most unlikely of places and not every "looked after" child who is unlikely ever to return to the birth family, comes from a background of impoverishment.

Similarly, even the most well-intentioned step-parent or partner of parent adoption may have the effect of removing the child from a prospective inheritance that a special guardianship order, child arrangements order or some other arrangement that does not break the link with one side of the child's family, would not.

Before making an adoption order the court must, under section 46 (6), consider whether there should be any contact arrangements. This issue is considered later.

The adopted child does not get a new birth certificate. What the adopters and the child receive is an extract from the register of adopted persons. There are two forms of extracts – the full form gives only the details of the child and the adopters – there is no reference back to the birth family or any previous names but it makes reference to the fact of adoption.

The short form of extract is, somewhat misleadingly, headed "Certificate of Birth" and makes no reference to the fact of adoption. It is as if designed to assist with the concealing of the existence of the adoption order – which is likely to be a dangerous course to take.

REVOCATION OF AN ADOPTION ORDER

The case of **Re W (Children) [2009] EWCA Civ 59** ("The Webster case") is as famous for its heart breaking outcome as for its consequences in pure law. The parents had three children removed and made the subject of orders leading to adoption as a result of findings that the middle child's fractures were "inflicted".

Years after the adoption orders had been made, the fourth child was born (the parents had fled to Eire to try to avoid care proceedings) and in those proceedings serious doubt was cast on the validity of the findings in respect of the injuries.

But for reasons of public policy, the Court of Appeal refused to set aside the adoption orders.

Despite the general rule, from the Webster case, that a court will not revoke an adoption order validly made, the case of **PK V MR & MRS K [2015] EWHC 2316 Fam,** suggests that in extreme circumstances, it may.

A fourteen-year old girl, had been adopted at the age of four and then, two years later, sent to Ghana to live with extended family members, where she was abused by them.

Having eventually returned to this country she located her biological parents and applied for the adoption order to be revoked and for her surname to revert to that of her birth mother.

Pauffley J, referring to the fact that public policy considerations usually militate against the revocation of adoption orders, found that the facts (unchallenged by the adopters, who only attended the first hearing and thereafter did not participate) were sufficient to justify the exception to this principle.

Referring to the Webster case, and **Re W (Inherent Jurisdiction: Permission Application: Revocation Application and Adoption Order) [2013] 2 FLR 1609**, she said that the only vehicle for such a step would be the use of the Inherent Jurisdiction and that only in exceptional circumstances could that process be used.

THE AGE OF THE "CHILD"

Section 49(4) of the 2002 Act explains that -

> *"An application for an adoption order may only be made if the person to be adopted has not attained the age of 18 years on the date of the application."*

It must be, therefore, that as long as the application is lodged a day or two before the attaining of 18, the application can then proceed. The ultimate adoption order, if it is made, will be made of an adult. This is confirmed by subsection 5 of section 49, which provides-

> "*References in this Act to a child, in connection with any proceedings (whether or not concluded) for adoption, (such as "child to be adopted" or "adopted child") include a person who has attained the age of 18 years before the proceedings are concluded.*"

CHAPTER ELEVEN
ADOPTION OR SPECIAL GUARDIANSHIP

The concept of special guardianship, inserted into the Children Act 1989 section 14 by section 115 of the 2002 Act, was, as the explanatory note to section 115 sets out-

> *"intended to meet the needs of children who cannot live with their birth parents, for whom adoption is not appropriate, but who could still benefit from a legally secure placement."*

It is not uncommon for it to be not entirely obvious, nor a matter of agreement, whether adoption is, actually, the most appropriate outcome. The case law is rich on the subject,

In **A Local Authority v Y & Z & Others [2006] 2FLR** the High Court refused to make an adoption order in favour of two sets of uncles and aunts as it was considered that the distorting effects of an inter-family adoption would be undesirable.

Continuing that theme, in **S v B and Newport City Council, Re K [2007] 1 FLR 1116,** Maternal Grandparents, with whom a child, now nearly 7, had been placed at 6 months old, applied for an adoption order, initially, and, after the commencement of the Act, a special guardianship order in the alternative. The local authority, which had obtained a final care order in December 2001, was neutral as to which order but saw no purpose in the care order continuing. Birth parents were volatile and had been the subject of section 34(4) orders.

Hedley J preferred special guardianship, citing the risk that adoption would *"significantly skew otherwise perfectly comprehensible and not unusual family relationships and structures"*. He also made Children Act prohibited steps and section 91(14) orders to curb any desire for contact, unofficial or by way of application.

He suggested that adoption orders in close family placements might only be suitable in cases where there had been "*physical or forensic aggression*". The Court of Appeal in the later cases of AJ and M-J took the view that this was not an appropriate "template".

Then, in three consecutive decisions on 7th February 2007, the Court of Appeal looked further at this issue.

In **Re S (Adoption Order or Special Guardianship Order)** [2007] **1 FLR 819** the six-year old girl who was the subject of the application had spent most of the past three years with the Appellant foster carer who now wanted adoption. The Court at first instance had made a special guardianship order, without a proper Children Act section14 A (11) report and without anyone addressing the new 2002 Act's welfare checklist – that was resolved by **Re S (Adoption Order or Special Guardianship Order) No 2 [2007] 1 FLR 855** and the court directing the filing of a report detailing the missing information. This decision clarified, in a way that is particularly helpful to the local authority, that where there is a plethora of other reports which cover most of the required areas these can simply be "cross referenced" in the special guardianship report which only needs to detail the areas not covered elsewhere. That does require, however, the author of the report to read all the other reports first.

The surrounding facts were highly unusual in that-

a) Mother had made remarkable steps since the proceedings commenced in transforming her life and lifestyle,

b) The mother and the foster carer had an excellent relationship and each wanted the other to remain a significant figure in the little girl's life whatever the outcome of the case,

c) Contact was well established and, again, would continue (it was eventually decided that monthly contact was appropriate),

d) The child wanted her mother to continue to be her mother and to remain living with the applicant but having regular contact with mother.

The Court of Appeal did not consider that this was a case where adoption was appropriate, preferring the first instance outcome, flawed though the process was by which that outcome was achieved in that particular case.

Re S was not about "skewing", however, but the cases of AJ and MJ were.

The Court of Appeal in both cases was dealing with applications to adopt by aunts and uncles ("horizontal skewing" rather than, (imagining a family tree,) "vertical skewing", where the suggested adoption is by grandparents).

In **Re AJ (Adoption Order or Special Guardianship Order) [2007] 1 FLR 507** the child concerned, a boy, had lived with paternal aunt and uncle since the age of 6 months, in 2001. A final care order was made in 2002 with a provision for direct parental contact of which roughly one in ten had actually been attended by the parents.

In November 2004 the local authority changed its plan to adoption. The carers were content with this but took the view that if an adoption order were not granted they did not want a special guardianship order, they would prefer the care order to remain. They considered the parents volatile and unpredictable. At first instance the judge agreed that the parents were unreliable and that special guardianship was not a viable alternative. He made an adoption order, encouraged by a view that the adopters would still promote a clear understanding of AJ's identity and were still open to the idea of contact.

In **Re M-J (Adoption Order or Special Guardianship Order) [2007] 1 FLR 691** the child concerned had been placed with mother's half-sister, with a view to adoption, by a local authority two years after a final care plan to reunite with mother after a drug and alcohol treatment course had finally had to be abandoned. The local authority applied, in October 2005, to free the child for adoption, the carer applied to adopt and the mother applied to discharge the care order inviting the court at final hearing (by which time the 2002 Act was well under way,) to make a special guardianship order. The gambit also used was for the mother to invite the court to make a Children Act section 91(14) direction as to any future contact – this was offered on an indefinite basis.

Even with that offer by the mother, the court, at first instance, did not feel that a special guardianship order would give the carer the security which she needed. It seems that the mother's application to discharge the care order (which she abandoned on the 2nd day of the hearing) had made the carer very anxious as to her half-sister's future intentions, and the court took the view that the mother was not fully reconciled to the "permanency" of the aunt's care.

While emphasising that each case has to be decided on its own merits, the Court of Appeal, which dealt with both cases on the same day indicated that the "skewing" argument had been over played in the parents cases in AJ and M-J and that the need to invite the court to make section 91(14) directions exposes a weakness in the special guardianship regime.

In **Re DF and GF [2014] EWHC 2607 (Fam)** the court dealt with this issue following removal of children, by now aged 3 and 15 years, from a relationship with a violent partner (and father of the younger child) by care orders. The three-year old had been returned to mother, who had covertly allowed contact with the birth father, contrary to all agreements in the case, and so the child was again removed and placed with an aunt and uncle (who had been adopters, earlier, of three boys).

The local authority applied for a placement order, seeking, ultimately, that the placement with the aunt and uncle would be adoptive. The mother, the Children's Guardian and the 15-year old all urged the court to make special guardianship orders.

Pauffley J, applying Re MJ and Re AJ, made placement orders, despite the Guardian's view, the Judge indicating that the mother's manipulative and deceitful behaviour risked the stability of the placement.

She followed AJ and MJ in determining that in an extended family placement the risk of "skewing" family relationships was not as great as had been suggested.

She made recommendations as to direct contact with mother and half-sibling but no section 26 order as to contact – the issue being left to the adopter's discretion.

The facts of N V B & Others [2013] EWHC 820 Fam are much more extreme. The father was serving life imprisonment for murdering mother and raping her 16-year old sister. The children, aged 9 and 3, were, immediately after the murder, placed with grandparents, who eventually separated. So the final application, for adoption, was by the grandmother alone, but supported by the local authority and the Guardian.

Father, who would be eligible for release before the younger child reached 18, argued that there should be a special guardianship order, and offered a Children Act section 91(14) order as well.

The Applicant agreed yearly indirect contact but not by way of any defined order, simply a mention in the recital.

Theis J made an adoption order, indicating that-

1. The fact that the case, (albeit that it started with an application for a residence application) had taken 3 years and 6 months to reach a final hearing was lamentable;

2. The father had been described as "highly dangerous and controlling". It was not appropriate for the grandmother to have to share parental responsibility in any way with her daughter's murderer.

3. While there is always an element of "skewing" of family relationships in extended family adoption, these children know of their situation and know of the relationships within their family.

Re N (A Child) (Adoption Order) [2014] EWFC 1491 related to a child now 5 years old, who had been born with severe disabilities, some of which would continue into adulthood. She had spent the first 7 months of her life in hospital and then went straight to the Applicants, as foster parents. The mother was a drug user who played no part in the case. The father had been having monthly contact and was strongly opposed to the Applicants' wish to adopt, arguing that special guardianship would be the correct order and that adoption was too draconian.

Father had concerns also that an adoption order would weaken his opposition to removal from the country as it reduced his chances of being able to argue as to respect for his family life. Moor J indicated that he was not at all influenced by that argument.

The father had behaved with complete courtesy to the prospective adopters throughout, and they, in turn, were content to provide four two-hour contacts to father and to paternal grandmother per year, while this was possible but they resisted the making of a contact order. The Children's Guardian supported the adoption application and opposed the suggestion that there should be a contact order, indicating that this would be too inflexible.

Moor J accepted that this was an exceptional case, and laid emphasis on the fact that the child's disabilities would last beyond the age of 18. This in particular rendered special guardianship inappropriate. Adoption would provide a family for this child for the rest of her life.

A similar outcome, for partly similar reasons, can be found in **Re A (Children) [2015] EWCA Civ 1254.**

In Re T (A Child: Adoption or Special Guardianship) [2017] EWCA Civ 1797, no party disputed that the baby, who had been placed with an aunt and uncle, should live anywhere else but with them until his majority. The aunt and uncle had been fostering two older half-brothers, (aged 5 & 6) who had a different father, with whom they have ongoing contact.

The issue was whether baby T, who had no relationship with his father, should be adopted, as the carers wished, or be the subject of special guardianship orders. The older half-siblings were to be made the subject of special guardianship orders within linked proceedings – no-one opposed that outcome.

The first instance recorder (a District Judge with a lot of care experience) decided that, despite the strong argument of a Guardian who much favoured the SGO route, that nothing else would better meet the baby's needs than adoption. The Guardian appealed.

The Court of Appeal (Jackson L.J. giving the lead judgment) agreed entirely with the first instance judgment, despite the unusual disparity of outcomes in respect of the three children. The Court referred back to Re S (Adoption Order or Special Guardianship Order) 2007 and Re MJ (Adoption Order or Special Guardianship Order) also 2007 which confirmed that an adoptive outcome is not necessarily ruled out in a placement within the birth family, despite the "skewing" argument.

CHAPTER TWELVE
ADOPTION SUPPORT

This is not just about money. In many cases the other types of support, namely-

- facilitating discussion about adoption
- assistance as to contact between birth families and the child, including mediation,
- therapy for the child,
- training for the adopters and, if necessary, respite care,
- helping if disruption of the placement threatens,

will all be of immense help.

An example of judicial concern at a perceived, possible lack of adoption support of a non-financial kind can be found in **Re M (Children) [2016] EWCA Civ 61.**

Two brothers, who had suffered appalling neglect, physical abuse and possibly sexual abuse, were removed from their parents at ages 4 and 2, had several foster care breakdowns, because of their behaviour.

Despite "unequivocal" internal assessments that said, because of the behaviour of the older boy to his brother, the two should be separated, the younger boy's teacher and her husband (a couple in their fifties) were so moved by the prospect of the impending separation that they offered a home to both. The local authority placed them both with them and ultimately agreed to their adoption. By then the boys were 10 and 7. The placement lasted a year, before the mother accepted that she had hit the older boy, but in order to deal with his behaviour while she was driving the car that was putting all of them in serious danger.

Care orders were made in respect of both boys. The parents appealed the order only in respect of the younger and less disturbed boy, arguing that, given proper support, they could still manage him.

King L.J. allowed the appeal. She said that, with the benefit of hindsight, the couple "*were unlikely ever to have been able to cope*" with the behaviour of the boys, particularly the older one. She was unhappy at the lack of consideration of what adoption support should have been offered and whether that might have resolved the problems, certainly in respect of the younger boy.

The case, she said, underlined the importance of the duty, on the local authority, set out in section 4 (1) of the Adoption and Children Act, to carry out a proper assessment of the need for adoption support.

FINANCIAL SUPPORT

But money helps as well and is an integral part of more and more adoptive placements, especially as the impetus grows to get more and more "harder to place" children and groups of children out of the looked after system and into adoptive homes.

In recognition of the paucity of adoption support that actually reaches adopters, whether that might be because of shortcomings in the realisation that the support is available, reluctance to seek help on the part of adopters, or ineptness by adoption agencies, the Government has set up the Adoption Support Fund which, for example, provides up to £2,500 per adopted child for specialist assessment and £5,000 per child for therapy.

Financial support is not at all a creation of the 2002 Act, in fact the regulations which govern these payments were enabled by the 1976

Adoption Act, despite the date of the regulations. They are the Adoption Support Services Regulations 2005, ("ASR").

The non-financial services listed above are set out in Regulation 3 of ASR, but the list begins with "*financial support payable under Part 3*" and for advisors, either to adopters or to local authorities, there are a number of potential pitfalls in these regulations.

CIRCUMSTANCES IN WHICH FINANCIAL SUPPORT IS PAYABLE.

Regulation 8 explains that this type of support is only payable :-

> *(a) where it is necessary to ensure that the adoptive parent can look after the child;*
>
> *(b) where the child needs special care which requires greater expenditure of resources by reason of illness, disability, emotional or behavioural difficulties or the continuing consequences of past abuse or neglect;*
>
> *(c) where it is necessary for the local authority to make any special arrangements to facilitate the placement or the adoption by reason of —*
>
> *(i) the age or ethnic origin of the child; or*
>
> *(ii) the desirability of the child being placed with the same adoptive parent as his brother or sister (whether of full or half-blood) or with a child with whom he previously shared a home;*
>
> *(d) where such support is to meet recurring costs in respect of travel for the purpose of visits between the child and a related person;*

(e) where the local authority consider it appropriate to make a contribution to meet the following kinds of expenditure—

(i) expenditure on legal costs, including fees payable to a court in relation to an adoption;

(ii) expenditure for the purpose of introducing an adoptive child to his adoptive parent;

(iii) expenditure necessary for the purpose of accommodating and maintaining the child, including the provision of furniture and domestic equipment, alterations to and adaptations of the home, provision of means of transport and provision of clothing, toys and other items necessary for the purpose of looking after the child.

All of the above are entitled "financial support".

Regulation 9 provides that in addition to all the regulation 8 items, there may be paid to adopters who up to the adoption were local authority foster parents of the child, "*an element of remuneration*".

But "remuneration" can only be paid if -

i. the decision to pay it was made before the adoption order was made,

ii. the adopters received that remunerative element in their fostering allowance, (Reg. 9 (1) and (2))

It can only be paid for 2 years after the adoption unless the local authority considers it necessary to continue to pay it "*having regard to the exceptional needs of the child or any other exceptional circumstances*".

So what is the difference between "financial support" paid periodically and "remuneration".

At first blush it looks as though "financial support" is really about payment for things, costs and special arrangements. Regulation 8 begins with an explanation that financial support is payable only "*where it is necessary to ensure that the adoptive parent can look after the child*" and then goes on to describe a lot of specific circumstances –but doesn't say anything as specific as "to help financially maintain the child on a week by week basis".

When the regulations turn to the question of financial support paid periodically Reg. 10 says that it may be paid in this way-

> *a. ...if it is provided to meet a need which is likely to give rise to a recurring expenditure; or*
>
> *b. in any other case.......if the local authority and the adopter agree, by instalments".*

Again, this might sound more like recurring specific costs, such as the cost of medication or school fees.

The fact is that many local authorities are interpreting this as permission to pay "maintenance", by way of a monthly allowance, often linked with, for example, a level 1 foster care allowance, less any amount of Child Benefit or Tax Credit payable by the Government in respect of the child. This is not "remuneration", or at least it isn't so described.

Financial Support ceases if the child-

i. leaves the adopters

ii. ceases full-time education or training and starts work,

iii. qualifies for income support or job seekers allowance,

iv. reaches the age of 18 "*unless he continues in full-time education or training, when it* *may* (my underlining) *continue until the end of the course or training he is then undertaking*"

"Remuneration", on the other hand, is the sort of additional payment, akin to a salary, that is paid to a foster carer because of the special circumstances of the fostering arrangement, often that the child's needs involve the carer giving up work.

CONDITIONS

The local authority can make the provision of financial support subject to any condition it considers appropriate including timescales or the purpose for which the support shall be utilised (ASR regulation 12(2)). If a condition is not complied with it may suspend payment and/or demand repayment (regulation 12(3)).

Here is where provision as to repayment of the cost of house extensions, and charges to secure this repayment, and similar provisions are justified. They require close liaison between Adoption Team and local authority lawyers.

The payment of periodical financial support cannot begin until an agreement has been signed confirming that the adopter will-

a) notify the authority of-

   i. change of address,

   ii. death of the child,

   iii. any of the triggers in Reg. 11 for cessation of payments,

   iv. a change in the financial circumstances of himself or the child, (Reg (12)(1)(a).

b) supply an annual written statement of-

   i. his financial circumstances,

   ii. the financial needs and resources of the child,

   iii. his address and confirmation that the child still lives there.

So there is obviously a major question mark over all of this adoption support funding. It is payable by the local authority as a matter of discretion. How long will it last, as compared with the certainty of foster care payments?

This is a minefield for all concerned. These are the tensions-

i. The local authority has a massive impetus to get looked after children adopted. The temptation to "sell" the concept of adoption is great.

ii. The ability to "sweeten" the package when the child, or sibling group is harder to place is specifically set out in the "*special arrangements to facilitate the placement for adoption*" provisions in regulation 8, (above);

iii. The "downside" that the financial support package is subject to review is not always emphasised, or, if it is, understood.

iv. There is no way the court can make an order about this – it is all about the local authority using its discretion appropriately.

CHAPTER THIRTEEN
CONTACT AFTER ADOPTION OR PLACEMENT ORDERS

A. CONTACT DURING "AUTHORITY TO PLACE"

Once the Adoption Agency is authorised, by agreement or order, to place a child for adoption, any provision for contact under the Children Act 1989 ceases to have effect (section 26 (1) of the 2002 Act). The whole of sections 8 and 34 of the Children Act disappear and the only contact order that can be made during the placement phase is an order under section 26 of the 2002 Act.

The disappearance of section 34(1) of the Children Act has major implications for the issue of contact between the child who was previously in care and the child who is now subject to "authority to place" for adoption, when it comes to parental contact. No longer does the local authority have an obligation to afford contact between child and parent. The dissatisfied parent can no longer rely on the fact that the local authority which wants to say "No" has to apply to the court and justify itself.

This shift of power makes it more than ever essential for the advisor of the parent (and, it is suggested, of the child) to scrutinise the plan for the child.

A typical case, where a child has gone through care proceedings, will involve at the outset a degree of direct contact which will enable an assessment of the relationship with the parent. Where the outcome is a placement order, the extent and frequency of contact will probably have declined roughly in proportion to the decrease in the parent's chances of a successful return of the child. It will often be that contact has, by the time of the care and placement order final hearing, reduced to weekly or even fortnightly. From there it will be common for the plan to be to further reduce it to, let us say, monthly.

Some plans, at this point, provide for contact to then cease after a certain period. Others will provide for contact only to finally cease once adopters have been identified and matched. Anyone who has read the judgment of Jackson J (as he then was) in **A & S v Lancashire County Council [2012] EWHC 1689 Fam** will understand how the cutting off from contact with its birth family of a child who is not subsequently adopted will lead to that child becoming a "statutory orphan". That is the expression that leading counsel for the young people in that case (the then Anthony Hayden QC) used and it was used by the Judge in his powerful judgment.

It may be that the local authority with a placement order is brimming with confidence as to the likelihood of success in home finding. It is suggested that this is no reason for a plan that risks the "statutory orphanage".

It is likely that, confronted by a section 26 contact application, with the consequent removal of all discretion if an order is granted, the local authority will consider amending its plan. If not -

A section 26 contact order can be applied for by-

1. The child or the Agency,
2. Any parent, relative or guardian; ("relative" is defined in section 144 as "*any grandparent, brother, sister, uncle or aunt, whether of the full blood or half blood or by marriage*".)
3. Anyone who prior to authority to place had a Children Act contact order;

4. Anyone with a residence (or "living with") section 8 Children Act order or who had care of the child pursuant to an Inherent Jurisdiction order.

5. Anyone given leave by the court to apply.

The court can make a section 26 order of its own motion when making a placement order (subsection 4) and MUST consider the issue of contact before such an order is made (section 27 (4)). It may well be that a well-drafted section within the parent's final evidence, headed "Contact after the making of a placement order" and hedged around with comments such as "while I hope the court will not make a placement order, however.." will enable the case to be set out without the need for a full, paper application. It is conceded that the best option would be, however, for a formal application to be made.

A section 26 order will have effect while the Agency is authorised to place and even once placement has happened (section 27 (1)) right up until the making of the adoption order.

This is one of the interesting and difficult features about contact orders during these stages in the child's progression. Very different considerations will apply, particularly in the case of an older child, where locating a placement may not be that easy, So the contact issue will have to accommodate very different circumstances – for example-

a) When the child continues to live with the same foster carers and the search for adopters, (possibly fruitless) goes on,

b) Once adopters are found and the exciting, but perhaps also unsettling stage of explanation and introduction goes on,

c) Once the child is placed and there are "honeymoon", settling in and no doubt "testing out" periods.

These very different backcloths to the child's life may well mean that, if a section 26 contact order is made, there may need to be one or more applications to the court for the issue of the appropriateness of the order to be reconsidered.

As the section 26 order is described by section 27(1) as having effect-

> "*while the adoption agency is authorised to place the child for adoption or the child is placed for adoption*",

- it is suggested that the Section 26 order will cease once the adoption order is made, although the 2002 Act does not make that explicitly clear.

The Agency has power to refuse contact in an emergency similar to that set out in section 34(6) of the Children Act (section 27 (2)), together with the power to vary and discharge a section 26 order (section 26 (1) (b).

The effect of all this is a framework that neatly parallels most of section 34 of the Children Act with the important exception of the "shall allow" provision and the consequent lack of need for a Children Act section 34(4) equivalent.

Are local authorities therefore almost always offering suitable contact plans? Or have many parents given up the ghost by this time?

For the parent (or the child's representative who is instructed to pursue the concept of post adoption contact) to miss out the section 26 stage is probably fatal to such a proposition, unless everyone explicitly accepts the desirability of it.

In the 2008 case of **Re P (A Child) [2008] EWCA Civ 535** (the case which dealt with the parallel search for adopters and long-term foster carers) the Court of Appeal specifically approved the making, at first instance, of a section 26 order so that the matter of contact, during a period where both adopters and long term foster carers were being sought, could remain a matter "*for the court rather than for the local authority*".

B. POST-ADOPTION CONTACT

Indirect contact

Most adoption agencies propose that adopters should be encouraged to provide a brief report as to the progress of the child, which is anonymised and forwarded to the former parents by the adoption agency. The process also generally provides for a similar passage of brief information about the birth family to go back to the adopters, again via the agency. This arrangement is virtually always voluntary, rather than by virtue of an order of the court (see **Re T (Minors)(Adopted Children: Contact [1996] Fam 34** for the exception to that norm). It goes by the name of "post box contact".

Post box contact depends on the birth parents remaining in touch with the adoption agency and the continuation of goodwill on all sides. It is by no means always long-lasting

Direct, or face to face contact, after adoption.

The layman might be surprised that this issue exists. Those undergoing the extensive training and counselling which adoption approval entails are encouraged to be open to the idea. When it comes to a placement, particularly of a very young child, the idea may not have such appeal to the home finding team, although cases exist where a child, whose welfare "requires" adoption, still also "requires" some degree of direct contact with an extended family member. It may well not be a parent. Often the relationship which a child of an age to be placed for adoption has with an older sibling or a grandparent poses a major dilemma for all concerned.

WHAT THE 2002 ACT PROVIDES

In subsection 5 of section 26 there could, originally, be found a provision which said that nothing in section 26 prevented a 1989 Children Act contact application being made at the same time as the application to adopt. Section 46 (6) was, until more recently, the only other mention of contact after the final adoption order and it merely provides that the court, before making an adoption order, must

> "*consider whether there should be arrangements for allowing any person contact with the child; and for that purpose the court must consider any existing or proposed arrangements and obtain any views of the parties to the proceedings.*"

That was it, for many years – these two provisions involved nine lines of print out of 150 sections, over 142 pages.

But in the 2014 Children and Families Act, section 9, we find a new framework to, perhaps belatedly, plug that gap. It amends section 51 of the 2002 Act by adding a new subsection A, which in s.51A (1), provides for the making of contact orders where-

a) an agency has placed, or was authorised to place a child for adoption, and

b) the court is making, or has made and adoption order.

So these provisions are about contact orders at or after the making of adoption orders where local authorities or other adoption agencies place a child for adoption.

The section then proceeds, in subsection 2, to refer to "named persons".

It provides that the court can order-

- the adopters to "*allow the child to visit or stay with the person named in the order under this section, or for the person named in that order and the child otherwise to have contact with each other,*"

But, on the other hand, the court can make an order which will prohibit-

> "*the person named in the order under this section from having contact with the child.*"

It could be argued that these provisions are remarkably similar to section 8 Children Act contact and prohibited steps orders.

As to who these "named persons" are, subsection 3 of section 51 (A), lists them as-

> "*(a) any person who (but for the child's adoption) would be related to the child by blood (including half-blood), marriage or civil partnership;*
>
> *(b) any former guardian of the child;*
>
> *(c) any person who had parental responsibility for the child immediately before the making of the adoption order;*
>
> *(d) any person who was entitled to make an application for an order under section 26 in respect of the child (contact with children placed or to be placed for adoption) by virtue of subsection (3)(c), (d) or (e) of that section;*
>
> *(e) any person with whom the child has lived for a period of at least one year.*

Those who can apply for either of these orders are, according to subsection 4-

> *"(a) a person who has applied for the adoption order or in whose favour the adoption order is or has been made,*
>
> *(b) the child, or*
>
> *(c) any person who has obtained the court's leave to make the application."*

The application for leave, by persons other than adopters or child, involves the court, according to subsection 5, considering –

> *(a) any risk there might be of the proposed application disrupting the child's life to such an extent that he or she would be harmed by it (within the meaning of the 1989 Act),*
>
> *(b) the applicant's connection with the child, and*
>
> *(c) any representations made to the court by—*
>
> *(i) the child, or*
>
> *(ii) a person who has applied for the adoption order or in whose favour the adoption order is or has been made.*

The court appears to be left with no discretion as to asking the adopters whether they wish to make representations. Is a court really going to be obliged to continually disturb adopters by seeking their views in a case of repeated "nuisance" applications for leave?

Subsection 6 allows the court to make section 51(A) orders of its own motion;

Subsection 8 provides that section 8 of the Children Act 1989 will no longer be available for this sort of purpose.

But will direct contact actually be ordered? The dilemma is often substantial.

Some generalisations, often sweeping, may help to highlight the anxieties which face the court-

1. Contact after adoption should perhaps be to maintain an existing and important relationship, not to create or necessarily even strengthen one.

2. Only a minority of birth parents are equipped to make post adoption contact meaningful and positive for the child; they are the ones who, by their conduct will not threaten the placement. The adoptive placement is sacrosanct. Contact often works far better when the adopters were formerly foster carers.

3. Sibling contact may appear less complicated and threatening to the placement than contact to birth parents but the opposite may be the case.

4. Contact issues are as relevant in Step- parent (or, as described in the 2002 Act, "partner of parent") adoptions as in ordinary adoption

5. There is a sort of "no order" principle, although operated in a different way to Children Act cases proper. To what extent will the courts force contact upon adopters? A few cases show us that there has, in the past, been great reluctance to do this.

Case Law

The foundation case is that of **Re C (Minors) (Adoption Order: Conditions) [1988] 2 FLR 159.** The case was obviously a pre- Children Act case which, therefore, talked about an adoption order with a "condition" as to contact, rather than an order, as being something which the courts were very reluctant to impose on adopters.

One might have thought that this elderly decision might have been an easy target for change – but apparently not.

In **Re T (Adoption: Contact) [1995] 2 FLR 251**, Butler Sloss J, as she was then, was faced with a situation where the adopters were not averse to the idea of direct contact completely, but there was a slight divergence as to the amount of contact which was to happen. She asked herself whether it was right for the court to "saddle" the adopters with a section 8 Children Act order, with its inherent risk of future litigation, or whether the court should leave the discretion in the hands of adopters who, after all, the court was going to deem to be the actual parents of the child.

In this case she left the discretion with the adopters and made no order

In **Re S (Contact Application by Sibling) [1998] 2 FLR 897** a child of 9 made her own application for leave to seek a contact order after adoption of her 7-year old brother some years before. Despite the evidence of a Child Psychologist in favour of contact, Charles J felt he had to leave the question to the discretion of the adopters and refused leave. This decision also confirmed that it is the interests of the child subject of the application which are given primacy over a child applicant.

See also the remarks of Wall LJ in **Re R (Adoption: Contact) [2006] 1 FLR 373**, a case decided before the implementation of the 2002 Act, where the court made it clear that the prospects of a court making a contact order in favour of a half-sister, after adoption, were so remote, because this would be such an unusual order to make, that the applicant fell at the leave hurdle.

In that case Wall J said-

> "*So contact is more common, but nonetheless the jurisprudence is, I think, clear. The imposition on prospective adopters of orders for*

contact with which they are not in favour is extremely, and remains extremely unusual."

The court went on to refer to **Re T (Minors)(Adopted Children: Contact) [1996] Fam 34,** where the court departed from the Re C standpoint in view of the resiling from an agreement as to indirect contact almost immediately upon the making of the adoption order and the adopters refusal to give any explanation for this change of mind. This was held to have been "unreasonable", which gave the court room to make a contact order.

That was the test which was applied, following Re T, in the Court of Appeal case of **Oxfordshire CC v X, Y and J [2010] EWCA Civ 581.** Here adopters had agreed to twice yearly progress reports but would not agree to give photos of the children to the birth parents, fearing that the parents would be able to identify the children. The first instance judge said he thought the likelihood of that being possible was minimal and ordered them to provide these photos. The Court of Appeal upheld the appeal of the adopters, who were supported by the Local Authority, on the basis that, as the court had not found the adopters "unreasonable" there was no basis to impose a contact order on them. Adopters were entitled to carry out the task of bringing up adopted children without anxiety about issues such as this.

In **Re T (A Child) [2010] Court of Appeal, 4th November 2010** the then President gave the main judgment in a case brought by a grand-mother for a post adoption contact order. The grandmother had sought to be a carer during the care and placement order proceedings and had eventually had a meeting with the adopters, which they had found "emotive and difficult".

The Annex A report had recommended indirect contact only – grand-mother said her understanding was that the local authority were in favour of some direct contact but that could not be verified.

The Court of Appeal held that the Judge at first instance had been right to dismiss grandmother's application as the child's welfare was paramount and the concern as to grandmother's wish for contact and its implications was inhibiting the adopters from "enjoying being the child's parents".

But, despite this powerful line of cases, all confirming the need not to impose contact orders on unwilling adopters, in **MF v London Borough of Brent and Others [2013] EWHC 1838 (Fam)** Ryder LJ made, what he called a "limited" contact order ("limited" only in that there were to be "only" 8 per year, to grandmother and a sister,) in the case of a 7 year old boy being adopted by his long term foster carer.

The adopter acknowledged the need for this contact and was prepared to support it. She simply wanted to have the final say should there be any possible disruption in years to come. This adopter had given "excellent care" and was an "impressive" witness, who was anxious about the effect on the child of the contact that she was still prepared to give. With a brief reference acknowledging the case law, the Judge decided, having admittedly changed his mind a number of times during the case, to impose an order on the adopter.

But since then in **The Prospective Adopters v FB & Others [2015] EWHC 297**, Moor J comprehensively ruled out post-adoption contact "by way of a shared care arrangement", as sought by a rather unrealistic mother, in respect of a child of 2, and indicated that nothing apart from "post box" contact would be appropriate.

He also referred to a number of authorities that indicated that the court should be reluctant to impose contact orders on unwilling adopters, including Re T and the Oxfordshire case. While he made passing reference to MB as well, it was only as to adoption generally and not as to the appropriateness of imposing a contact order.

Moor J said-

> "*There are significant challenges to introducing contact when the child has no memory of the birth parent. It requires a high level of management. It can be very confusing and distressing to the child. The adopters would, in general, be expected to make the arrangements. This can cause difficulty in managing the emotions of the birth family so as to protect the boundaries of the adoptive family. In a serial number adoption, such as here, this would almost certainly lead to a lifting of the veil of anonymity.*"

He also said –

> "*It remains extremely unusual to impose a contact order on prospective adopters which they are not in agreement with.*"

MORE BOOKS BY LAW BRIEF PUBLISHING

A selection of our other titles available now:-

'A Practical Guide to Vicarious Liability' by Mariel Irvine
'A Practical Guide to Claims Arising from Delays in Diagnosing Cancer' by Bella Webb
'A Practical Guide to Applications for Landlord's Consent and Variation of Leases' by Mark Shelton
'A Practical Guide to Relief from Sanctions Post-Mitchell and Denton' by Peter Causton
'Butler's Equine Tax Planning: 2nd Edition' by Julie Butler
'A Practical Guide to Equity Release for Advisors' by Paul Sams
'A Practical Guide to Immigration Law and Tier 1 Entrepreneur Applications' by Sarah Pinder
'A Practical Guide to Unlawful Eviction and Harassment' by Stephanie Lovegrove
'In My Backyard! A Practical Guide to Neighbourhood Plans' by Dr Sue Chadwick
'A Practical Guide to the Law Relating to Food' by Ian Thomas
'A Practical Guide to the Ending of Assured Shorthold Tenancies' by Elizabeth Dwomoh
'Commercial Mediation – A Practical Guide' by Nick Carr
'A Practical Guide to Financial Services Claims' by Chris Hegarty
'The Law of Houses in Multiple Occupation: A Practical Guide to HMO Proceedings' by Julian Hunt
'A Practical Guide to Unlawful Eviction and Harassment' by Stephanie Lovegrove
'A Practical Guide to Solicitor and Client Costs' by Robin Dunne
'Artificial Intelligence – The Practical Legal Issues' by John Buyers
'A Practical Guide to Wrongful Conception, Wrongful Birth and Wrongful Life Claims' by Rebecca Greenstreet

‘Occupiers, Highways and Defective Premises Claims: A Practical Guide Post-Jackson – 2nd Edition’ by Andrew Mckie

‘A Practical Guide to Financial Ombudsman Service Claims’ by Adam Temple & Robert Scrivenor

‘A Practical Guide to the Law of Enfranchisement and Lease Extension’ by Paul Sams

‘A Practical Guide to Marketing for Lawyers – 2nd Edition’ by Catherine Bailey & Jennet Ingram

'A Practical Guide to Advising Schools on Employment Law' by Jonathan Holden

'Certificates of Lawful Use and Development: A Guide to Making and Determining Applications' by Bob Mc Geady & Meyric Lewis

'A Practical Guide to the Law of Dilapidations' by Mark Shelton

‘A Practical Guide to the 2018 Jackson Personal Injury and Costs Reforms’ by Andrew Mckie

‘A Guide to Consent in Clinical Negligence Post-Montgomery’ by Lauren Sutherland QC

‘A Practical Guide to Running Housing Disrepair and Cavity Wall Claims: 2nd Edition’ by Andrew Mckie & Ian Skeate

‘A Practical Guide to the General Data Protection Regulation (GDPR)’ by Keith Markham

‘A Practical Guide to Digital and Social Media Law for Lawyers' by Sherree Westell

‘A Practical Guide to Holiday Sickness Claims – 2nd Edition’ by Andrew Mckie & Ian Skeate

‘A Practical Guide to Inheritance Act Claims by Adult Children Post-Ilott v Blue Cross’ by Sheila Hamilton Macdonald

‘A Practical Guide to Elderly Law’ by Justin Patten

‘Arguments and Tactics for Personal Injury and Clinical Negligence Claims’ by Dorian Williams

‘A Practical Guide to QOCS and Fundamental Dishonesty’ by James Bentley

‘A Practical Guide to Drone Law’ by Rufus Ballaster, Andrew Firman, Eleanor Clot

‘Practical Mediation: A Guide for Mediators, Advocates, Advisers, Lawyers, and Students in Civil, Commercial, Business, Property, Workplace, and Employment Cases’ by Jonathan Dingle with John Sephton

'Practical Horse Law: A Guide for Owners and Riders' by Brenda Gilligan
'A Comparative Guide to Standard Form Construction and Engineering Contracts' by Jon Close
'A Practical Guide to Compliance for Personal Injury Firms Working With Claims Management Companies' by Paul Bennett
'A Practical Guide to the Landlord and Tenant Act 1954: Commercial Tenancies' by Richard Hayes & David Sawtell
'A Practical Guide to Personal Injury Claims Involving Animals' by Jonathan Hand
'A Practical Guide to Psychiatric Claims in Personal Injury' by Liam Ryan
'Introduction to the Law of Community Care in England and Wales' by Alan Robinson
'A Practical Guide to Dog Law for Owners and Others' by Andrea Pitt
'Ellis and Kevan on Credit Hire – 5th Edition' by Aidan Ellis & Tim Kevan
'RTA Allegations of Fraud in a Post-Jackson Era: The Handbook – 2nd Edition' by Andrew Mckie
'RTA Personal Injury Claims: A Practical Guide Post-Jackson' by Andrew Mckie
'On Experts: CPR35 for Lawyers and Experts' by David Boyle
'An Introduction to Personal Injury Law' by David Boyle
'A Practical Guide to Claims Arising From Accidents Abroad and Travel Claims' by Andrew Mckie & Ian Skeate
'A Practical Guide to Cosmetic Surgery Claims' by Dr Victoria Handley
'A Practical Guide to Chronic Pain Claims' by Pankaj Madan
'A Practical Guide to Claims Arising from Fatal Accidents' by James Patience
'A Practical Approach to Clinical Negligence Post-Jackson' by Geoffrey Simpson-Scott
'A Practical Guide to Personal Injury Trusts' by Alan Robinson
'Employers' Liability Claims: A Practical Guide Post-Jackson' by Andrew Mckie
'A Practical Guide to Subtle Brain Injury Claims' by Pankaj Madan
'The Law of Driverless Cars: An Introduction' by Alex Glassbrook
'A Practical Guide to Costs in Personal Injury Cases' by Matthew Hoe

'A Practical Guide to Alternative Dispute Resolution in Personal Injury Claims – Getting the Most Out of ADR Post-Jackson' by Peter Causton, Nichola Evans, James Arrowsmith
'A Practical Guide to Personal Injuries in Sport' by Adam Walker & Patricia Leonard
'The No Nonsense Solicitors' Practice: A Guide To Running Your Firm' by Bettina Brueggemann
'Baby Steps: A Guide to Maternity Leave and Maternity Pay' by Leah Waller
'The Queen's Counsel Lawyer's Omnibus: 20 Years of Cartoons from The Times 1993-2013' by Alex Steuart Williams

These books and more are available to order online direct from the publisher at www.lawbriefpublishing.com, where you can also read free sample chapters. For any queries, contact us on 0844 587 2383 or mail@lawbriefpublishing.com.

Our books are also usually in stock at www.amazon.co.uk with free next day delivery for Prime members, and at good legal bookshops such as Hammicks and Wildy & Sons.

We are regularly launching new books in our series of practical day-to-day practitioners' guides. Visit our website and join our free newsletter to be kept informed and to receive special offers, free chapters, etc.

You can also follow us on Twitter at www.twitter.com/lawbriefpub.

www.ingramcontent.com/pod-product-compliance
Lightning Source LLC
LaVergne TN
LVHW022104200926
848481LV00003B/1059
9781912687190